LIFE
from the
INSIDE
UP

Why live a godly life?

MARK R. LITTLETON

ACCENT BOOKS
Denver, Colorado

Unless otherwise noted, all Scripture references taken from the *Holy Bible, New International Version*. Copyright © 1973, 1978, 1984 International Bible Society. Used by permission of Zondervan Bible Publishers.

ACCENT BOOKS

A division of Accent Publications
12100 West Sixth Avenue
P.O. Box 15337
Denver, Colorado 80215

Library of Congress Catalog Card Number 90-84820

ISBN 0-89636-266-3

For
the men of my Christian Businessmen's Committee:
Joe, Carey, Curt, Fred, Steve, Lee, Watson, Paul, Dan, Chip
whose lives count and who have counted for much in
my life.
You've taught me to want to excel.

CONTENTS

"No eye has seen, no ear has heard, no mind has conceived what God has prepared for those who love him. . . ."

(1 Corinthians 2:9)

"And this is my prayer: that your love may abound more and more in knowledge and depth of insight, so that you may be able to discern what is best and may be pure and blameless until the day of Christ."

(Philippians 1:9-10)

"To him who is able to keep you from falling and to present you before his glorious presence without fault and with great joy."

(Jude 24)

Introduction

Disappointment with God Revisited

Of late I have read a number of deeply disturbing books. *Disappointment with God* by Phillip Yancey provided insight and illumination. Many of my own feelings of disillusionment as a Christian with high expectations were exposed and touched. As one who often longs to see God do something "so big the world will know He did it," Yancey provided a potent word.

The Lie of the Good Life by Alice S. Lawhead also knocked some holes in my sometimes effervescent theology and belief that God will make my life turn out well. As I read the stories and laments of women bashed up and crunched by life like steaming wrecks on the fence of the Indianapolis 500 speedway, I found myself identifying with their feelings of despair and betrayal. Christ came to give us "life abundant." But where is it? What has gone wrong?

We seem to have fallen into a psychoanalyzing mode where we pile our grievances, disillusionments, lack of passion, anger, and bitterness before God and shriek, "Okay, there it is. We've told you how we feel! Now what are *you* going to do about it?"

But is all this scrape-my-psyche, lacerate-my-spirit psycho-dialysis good? Are we helping ourselves by ventilating these spasms of fury?

I'm not trying to be mean-spirited or insensitive. I have experienced passion as a Christian. I have experienced intense despair and disillusionment in my walk with God also.

In the midst of it all, life has been a roller coaster ride of ups, downs, and arounds that I can hardly understand or piece together. Sometimes I ask, "The 'abundant life'—what's that?" "Love, joy, peace, patience" etc.—the fruit of the Spirit—who lives it consistently? "God works all things for good." Yes, I believe it. But I can hardly see how "all things" have worked that way. I trust it's true and one day I may see it as God sees it. But for the most part, I've found my idea of "all things" and "good" rarely conforms to what has happened.

Frankly, much of the hype about the Christian life is simply not true. To be a Christian in this world means being a soldier in a conflict as gritty, mean, nasty, brutal, and painful as serving in Patton's division during the Battle of the Bulge. The real rewards of Christian living are not in the here and now; rather, God has reserved them for eternity.

That doesn't mean we can't experience joy, goodness, love, and hope right now. We do. I do. But happy and fleeting emotions are not what life is all about. Jesus said a lot more about perseverance and hanging in there than He did about joyous spasms of praise. He spoke more about gut-wrenching fasting, sweat-weary prayer, and pain-inducing sacrifice than the idea of a happy lark in the park of Planet Earth.

I'm learning that much of Christian faith calls us to think about God's promises for heaven and the future, and not to fix our eyes on what we want in this world. When we do set our hopes on this life on any level—material, emotional, even spiritual—we often end up vastly disappointed. Middle class Americans in particular suffer from this malady. Because we do have so much—nice homes, decent family lives, money to spend in restaurants—we lose sight of the fact that this world is a graveyard, and the offerings of this world worthless in the eyes of God. If God meant it to be easy down here and "life abundant" as we would like to understand it, then why did He curse our race and our planet to pain in childbirth, lack of fulfillment in our work, and final disintegration in death?

I'm not trying to be negative, but all this has led me to the belief that heaven's rewards are not something to be sneered at, passed over, scorned, ignored, or treated lightly. In fact, understanding God's rewards and why He gives them can reenergize a life, giving us new passion and fortitude perhaps like nothing else. When we see that this world isn't the end, and what we do in this world has an impact on the next, something changes inside us.

We're talking about accolades spoken before the whole gathering of heaven. We're referring to privileges that the President of the United States would give up his job for. We're speaking of joys and special gifts that make Donald Trump's billions look like shortcake.

What's more, it's all available to each of us. None of us has to convert a million souls, write four bestsellers, win "theologian of the year," or make the cover of *TIME* to qualify. All we have to be are humble, fervent Christians, committed to God's work, Christians who seek to obey Him and to carry out our responsibilities with faith and perseverance.

This has nothing to do with salvation. Salvation and eternal life are gifts, gained only through genuine faith in Christ as our sin-bearer and redeemer (Ephesians 2:8-9).

However, our "works" do matter to God (James 2). How we conduct and live our lives now bears consequences for eternity. I can't fritter away my time, money, and family life figuring that because I'm saved it will all turn out right in the end. I'd rather know now what God says matters so that I can begin doing it, rather than find out too late that I've given my life to goals, ideals, and attitudes that will end in ashes...and ultimately fail to live for Him for all the todays He gives me (I Corinthians 3:10-15).

I'm also afraid that our "instant gratification society" can't see beyond today. "Who cares about the sweet bye and bye? I want mine now, and I want it big."

9

But no Christian has to live with that kind of mentality—or its resulting anxiety. Our lives can count for good, for joy, forever—starting right now. Each of us has the power to begin laying up treasures in heaven that will look like a personal diamond mine. The world may not notice any of what we've done. But the Lord assures us there are activities, sacrifices, gifts, and services that we can all do which win His praise. I, for one, want to invest my life in those things.

This promise of rewards is a powerful motivator. Knowing that in heaven we will receive a hundred times what we sacrificed on earth in His name should spur us on to greater service and devotion to Christ. Jesus even used this truth as an encouragement to His own disciples (Matthew 19:27-29). Some families choose missions over Wall Street and sacrificial giving over buying a new Mercedes because God says He will reward such choices. When I have opened the check book at times to pay bills and also give to Christian organizations, the fact of God's promise encourages me. It's not for nothing. It's not pie in the sky. It's not a hype dream. Those sacrifices count—both now and for eternity.

God assures each of us—no matter what our station, position, locale, or gifts—that we can live lives and do deeds that impact our future in heaven.

As we set our minds on the things above, the rewards God promises, and the actions that generate those rewards (I John 2:15-17; Colossians 3:1-4), we can begin giving our lives to what really matters. Knowing that we're giving our lives to something that lasts will help us tough it out.

Frankly, that's what I need—strength to "tough it out." Life is not easy. Its difficulties sting. Too much of it seems like pain and hassles that never end. But one day it will. And one day, those who are rich in faith will be handsomely rewarded by Him whose reward is literally "out of this world."

Knowing that makes it all worth it. I hope as you read you will discover a new sense of direction, hope, and commitment to our

Savior. What we do now counts. There are consequences that impact eternity. And it can be for good, for glory, for grace and praise forever!

Mark Littleton
Columbia, Maryland

SECTION ONE:
The Great Question

-1-

Are We Running Off in Every Direction?

The hurry level is going up in America. It used to be that if you missed the stagecoach in the Old West, you simply sighed, went home, and figured you'd catch it next month. Today, if a person misses a section of the subway turnstile, he's ready to kill. In fact, we're hearing of people actually shooting it out on the byways and highways of California. And whatever happens there soon happens elsewhere.

I noticed it this morning as I brushed my teeth. My train of thought went something like this: "It takes me about 40 seconds to brush my teeth. If I could brush faster, I might knock off 10, maybe 15 seconds. Then I could get out that much sooner to type on the word processor."

Now what I want to know is: Am I crazy or just dentally-retarded?

After that, during my drive to work, I thought I might show a little aeronautical mettle and "push the envelope a little closer to the edge"—get to where I was going that much faster. However, a policeman was behind me—another time buster—and I had to go by regular mail rather than express.

Commercials on television often appeal to our need to get things done now, this very moment, and not a second later. Some entrepreneurs even feature "Same Day Service"—if you get up early enough and have the presence of mind at that hour to use it.

However, when it comes to mail, some of us would just settle for "same city" service or even "same package delivered as sent" service.

At my bank I used to have to wait until the next business day to cash my check. No more. I can cash my check any time, 24 hours a day, thanks to computerized checking. All I need now is the money for which to cash such checks.

In the midst of all this high performance, a prophet will pop up occasionally and counsel us all to meander a bit and smell the roses. I take such advice to heart, too. Each time I pass a rose I make a quick jerk in its direction, sniff, let go an ecstatic sigh, and then glance around to see if any of the scurrying masses noticed my deed. But most of them just hurry by, or bump into me and shout, "Watch where you're sniffing, buster."

One might think that Christians could overcome such worldly attitudes. But we're not immune to this helter skelter sprint toward our destiny either. We want to hurry up and get spiritual, get success, get a wife, get a husband, get what we want when we want it—and with a smile, please.

Then along comes someone like you or me who pauses in our heart-long sprint into whatever and we ask, "What am I doing with my life?" We're frittering it away a week at a shot. At the end, we're afraid we could look back and see nothing of value.

If you're like me, you pray about it. But impatience can jam the lines here, too. "Lord, I'm too tense and irritable. Slow me down—immediately!"

You might memorize Ephesians 5:16 which tells us to "make the most of our time." So you go out and buy a new alarm clock guaranteed to awaken you at 5:30 a.m. so you can have a quiet time like John Wesley did. Or you find a little out of the way alcove at work to catch some winks on your lunch break.

The rat race is getting rattier every day, isn't it? Do you ever feel as though you've gone off in all directions?

What counts, anyway?

Does it really matter that I took five extra minutes today being nice to one of those fellows I manage at the plant? No one seemed to notice, not even him. Does it matter to God that I spent 30 minutes this morning reading Ephesians? Even my wife doesn't applaud that one because she knows I'll be dead tonight at nine-thirty. Does it count in heaven that I teach those junior boys in Sunday School? I don't feel like I'm accomplishing anything—except getting more adept at dodging spitballs. Sometimes I feel like saying, "What's the use?"

Have you ever asked that question? Does God care that I stopped in traffic and prayed, even if what I prayed was, "Please let this traffic jam pass quickly"? Did He notice that I gave my wife an extra hug and kiss tonight? Was He pleased with the fact that I studied so hard preparing for this Sunday's class? Does any of it count for anything in this world or beyond this world? Am I fooling myself?

The Scriptures warn us repeatedly that one day we'll give an account of our lives to Christ (Romans 14:12). That's difficult enough to swallow. But many of us, as we scrutinize the way things are going, might justifiably ask, "Will any of it last? Am I doing anything for which He might tell me, 'Well done'?"

Plainly, if we're thinking at all, we'd better find out what does matter, or we may end up losing everything. We know we can't take anything with us. And there are great spiritual and personal rewards in this life, but *can* we send anything on ahead?

I tend to think that a job well done has its own satisfaction. But, frankly, I haven't seen that many jobs well done lately. In fact, most of them are jobs partly done, or undone, or jobs I wish I didn't have to do!

What matters? The bottom line? A promotion? Productivity? Higher profits? Memorizing Scripture verses? Reading through the Bible in one year? Leading someone to Christ?

What on earth matters in heaven? If an angel slid down and

15

murmured in my ear what I should give myself to today, what would he say?

Martin Luther once said that if he didn't give the first three hours of his morning to prayer, Satan got the victory for the rest of his day.

John Wesley remarked that he wanted to live his life as if he would die tonight.

Jim Elliott wrote, "He is no fool who gives what he cannot keep to gain what he cannot lose."

Vince Lombardi remarked, "Winning is everything."

Who's right? What matters—really?

PLENTY!

Few of us weigh the meaning of heaven and its rewards against what we see in this life. Often, we're just happy to make it through the day. As we visit Mom at the nursing home, or give an employee a pat on the back, or sit down with a daughter to listen to her pour out her troubled story, we rarely consider that such things might make an honorable mention in heaven. After all, regardless of God's rewards, isn't it right to do those things because we're Christians?

Certainly. But each of us also knows that the battle between good and bad, nice and decent and loving is life's most profound struggle. Too often when there's good to be done, we end up feeling we "blew it" rather than rejoicing that we helped.

So why do we seek to grow in our Christian walk? To obey God's commands? To serve the church? To love our spouses, children, friends, and neighbors? Why do we witness? Pray? Watch what we say? Seek to grow the fruit of the Spirit?

Isn't there something in each of us that wants—wishes— even hopes—that when we appear before Christ, He'll have something good to say about our lives? Wouldn't it be encouraging to hear Jesus say one day, "You did a good job with what I gave you to work with and what you were up against. Well done."

It's the idea of rewards that turns my head around. When the Bible assures me that one day God will "recompense me for the deeds done in the body" (II Corinthians 5:10, NASB) and He'll give a "crown of righteousness" (II Timothy 4:8) to those who longed for Christ coming, I think, "I've got to get my mind off this world!"

Of course you say, "That's so obvious, Mark. Didn't you ever read the Scripture that says, 'Lay up treasure in heaven' or 'Seek first His righteousness...and all these things will be added to you'?"

Sure I have! But that doesn't make the glamor, fame, wealth, and glory of this world any less glittery. I can see the Super Bowl champions on TV. It's far more difficult to imagine a heaven described in only a few verses in the Bible.

Someone said to me recently, "When I was in college, all I thought about was Bible studies, leading friends to Christ, and serving the Lord. But you know, now that I'm married, with three kids, a mortgage, two gas-guzzling cars, and a horde of bills to pay, all I think about is, 'Please give me a raise at work, Lord'."

The problems of this existence can stifle our spiritual sensibilities until life becomes little more than a terrifying traipse through enemy territory. If only I knew that what I was doing for the Lord—reading my Bible, teaching a class, trying to live a godly life—held out the promise of something special. I'd prefer my rewards now, but maybe His personal gift to me, in the eternal life of heaven, is worth sticking it out...just for its own sake.

That's what this book is all about. Encouragement. If we're born again, our life counts in God's eyes. He made us for a purpose. Even though we may feel like we don't add up to much next to the biggies—Billy, Chuck, Karen, Shirley, Jim, and the rest—don't worry! God doesn't measure our lives against one another. We're not in competition. It's possible to fill our lives with thoughts, words, and deeds that please God and will win

His acclaim and approval, as well as some choice responsibilities and privileges in heaven.

ARE YOU MAKING YOUR LIFE COUNT?

Let me give you a test.

Question One: Do you know what counts in God's eyes? What Scriptures would you use as a basis for answering such a question?

I remember sitting in a hospital room with a man on the brink of despair and even suicide. I'll call him Al. He peered at me with wet eyes and said, "My life has been a total waste. I've done nothing God would consider worthy. You know the passage that says a person's life will go through the fire and some people will end up with everything being burned up? That's me: Ashes Al."

I tried to find a word of encouragement, but I could think of nothing. Then a nurse came in. She adjusted some equipment, smoothed his pillow, and touched my friend's forehead, saying, "Feel any better today, Mr. _____ ?"

He nodded. "You've really made me feel better, ma'am. Thanks a lot. If I had a daughter, I'd've loved for her to be like you."

The nurse nodded, but I noticed her eyes mist, then she went out. After she was gone, I said, "Al, you just did something that counts in God's eyes."

He grimaced incredulously. "What?"

"The Scripture says we'll give an account of our words when we stand before Jesus. And what you just said to that nurse certainly would win Jesus' approval, don't you think?"

He appeared amazed, then chagrined. "If that's so, then why don't I do it more?"

"That's just the point," I said. "You should do it more. Knowing that words of encouragement, uplift, and love count in God's eyes will make you want to let it fly."

He laughed. "Well, man, that's simple. I can do that all day."

I nodded. It doesn't have to be complicated to count with God.

If you don't know what God says makes waves in heaven, how can you even quiver the waters? When we know what matters in God's eyes, we can begin to pursue those kind of words, deeds, and thoughts consciously.

Question Two: Does it matter to you what God wants? Do you want to please God, or is that a dead (or dumb) issue?

Sometime ago my six-year-old and I were having a little father-daughter dispute. She wanted to play with her bunnies. I pushed for a major room clean up. After several demands, pretenses, and tricks, I finally said, "Nicole, do you want to please me and make me want to give you every blessing under the sun?"

Her eyes were wide. "Yes, Daddy."

"Do you know how you can do that?"

"How?"

"By doing what I say."

"What if I don't?"

I had to think about that one. "Well, I'll still love you. But I won't be happy with you. Do you want me to be happy with you?"

She nodded her head.

"Then what will make me happy right now is you cleaning up your room."

She hopped to it.

You may be thinking, "That's an awful example of parental manipulation, Mark."

I think of manipulation as a tricky way to wangle someone into doing something they really don't want to do. All I told her was the truth: what I desired and the fact that her obeying me mattered to me and would gain my blessing. I don't believe that was manipulation; it was honesty and forthrightness.

In the same way, God desires that *we* will *want* to please Him. And He has offered us a Bible full of ways.

19

Question three: If you knew what counts in God's eyes, would you begin doing it?

The perennial pastoral question: *Will you do it?* So simple, yet so profound.

In a meeting in our company, we discussed a problem that no one could solve. No one took personal responsibility for the solution, so we were all passing the memo. At the end of the meeting—after we'd defined the problem, broken it down into increments, assigned parts to everyone concerned—our fearless leader stopped us all in our tracks. He looked each of us fiercely in the eye and asked, "Who is planning right now not to follow through?"

No one said a word.

"Then, gentlemen," he said, "it's as good as solved. Now go do your part."

"Your part." Afterward I thought what a nice expression that is. That means it's not all on me. I'm not the only one responsible. We can lean on one another. This is a team effort.

That's all God asks. "Just do your part."

"And?"

"And," He says, "I'll reward you handsomely" (II Corinthians 5:10).

That's more than enough for me.

SECTION TWO:
We Will All Stand Before Christ

-2-
God Wants to Reward Us!

Summers can be agony for mothers. The kids simply don't know what to do with themselves. "What can I do now, Mom?"

"Color in your coloring book."

"I already did that."

"Go out in the yard and throw a ball."

"With who?"

"With whom."

"Who?"

"Forget it. Go find John and play out in the yard."

"He went on vacation."

"Then go to Billy's. I saw him outside this morning."

"We had a fight."

Mom grits her teeth, gazes forlornly at the once clean house that's now a carnage, and sighs. "How about if we make some cookies?"

"What kind?"

"Oatmeal."

"Yuck."

Finally, she throws up her arms and says, "I don't know what to tell you to do. BUT GET OUT OF HERE!"

My mom, though, never tore her hair out. She had a trick. Swim team. Every summer morning from 9 to 12 a.m. I and my siblings meandered up to the local pool and flailed out our frustrations under the tutelage of Mr. Rhea, a hard core member

21

of the coaching fraternity who believed, "You haven't worked out until we pull you out with a rope."

Frankly, I hated swim team. I'm convinced someone threw chunks of ice into the pool each morning before we got there. My skin numbed just thinking about it. And Mr. Rhea never let up. There were wind sprints, long distance, butterfly, breaststroke, backstroke, and 10 extra laps if you were caught loafing. He even used this one maneuver where you tied strips of inner tube rubber around your legs and hands and had to swim like a dolphin. I distinctly remember drowning twice performing that one.

Still, there was one thing good about swim team: ribbons and trophies. Every Saturday we had a "meet." If you swam and came in anywhere from first to fifth place (and there were only eight lanes) you won a colorful ribbon with your place written on it. I collected a few of those ribbons and stuck them on my bulletin board by my desk. Somehow those inexpensive little glimmers of green and red enabled me to endure Mr. Rhea, the freezing pool, and the indignities of tying my feet together with inner tube rubber. I wanted as many of them as I could get.

It's a funny thing about such rewards. You can be eight or eighty, yet most of us go for them. Whether it's "Bowling for Dollars," swimming for ribbons, or batting for balls, they motivate us like nothing else. Winning something and making a mark is important to all of us. We want to be recognized for something, some achievement. Perhaps it's something God Himself has put inside of us, some part of our psyche that craves recognition, respect, being known as "somebody."

IS WANTING A REWARD WRONG?

Is it wrong to want a reward for work well done, to long to excel and gain recognition? Many Christians would say such an attitude is the very opposite of true humility.

Perhaps, but then why has God spoken of rewards so consistently and liberally throughout Scripture? It's only when we pervert those desires so that they become lusts—like when the desire for food turns to gluttony or the need for recognition becomes pride—that we stumble into sin.

To desire God's recognition, respect, and approval is a godly, healthy desire. It drives us to strive and endure in a hard race known as life.

Eric Heiden, the winner of five gold medals in the 1980 Winter Olympics, spent hours every day in weight-training, skating, and racing. He poured his energies into his discipline from the early years of his life. It became one monumental obsession. Winning the gold was everything.

A friend keeps a plaque in his office with words written by Vince Lombardi, the famed Green Packers coach and winner of several football world championships. He said, "Wining isn't everything; it's the only thing." He pursued the number one slot so relentlessly that he often drove himself and his men to exhaustion on the football field.

These men had a passion. Do we as Christians have the same kind of passion that drives us to advance God's work and righteousness? Like Jesus said, "But seek first his kingdom and his righteousness, and all these things will be given to you as well" (Matthew 6:33).

IT'S LIKE A RACE

Paul often used the analogy of the athletic field. He told Timothy, "If anyone competes as an athlete, he does not receive the victor's crown unless he competes according to the rules" (II Timothy 2:5). He informed the Corinthians that, "Everyone who competes in the games goes into strict training. They do it to get a crown that will not last; but we do it to get a crown that will last forever" (I Corinthians 9:25). Anyone who masters a sport knows the price you must pay. It's sheer, driving pain for hours a day. Paul knew how an athlete had to expend himself and that this life is the training field for heaven.

In another passage, Paul spoke more specifically of the

Christian race. He told Timothy, "I have fought the good fight, I have finished the race, I have kept the faith. Now there is in store for me the crown of righteousness, which the Lord, the righteous Judge, will award to me on that day—and not only to me, but also to all who have longed for his appearing" (II Timothy 4:7-8). It was a fight, a race. He knew the grueling laps, the wind sprints, the burn in the legs. But he drove for the tape as though nothing but winning mattered...winning the Lord's approval and the, "Well done, thou good and faithful servant."

Of course, there is a distinction between winning in a worldly arena and winning in God's eyes. On earth, it's man and woman pitted against each other. But in the heavenly realm, it's not that way at all.

THE GOOD FIGHT

Notice what Paul says he competed against. He "fought the good fight." He didn't battle against other people. He fought against sin, the flesh, and the devil; he fought the battle to obey the Lord and overcome the forces of Satan. He sought to fight a "good" rather than a "bad" fight. God would reward him on the basis of how he pummeled the evil in his life, not other Christians, and how he obeyed God.

FINISHING THE COURSE

Paul refers to the second element when he says, "I have finished the race" (II Timothy 4:7). Again, it's a graphic picture. Paul ran a course which symbolized his whole Christian life. His goal was to finish it, faith and commitment intact.

What is that course? He encapsulized it in Ephesians 2:10: "For we are God's workmanship, created in Christ Jesus to do good works; which God prepared in advance for us to do." God created us for "good works." He prepared them before He created the world. For each one of us, He has laid out a course. On Sunday, He placed one good work in our path. On Monday,

24

it was another. And on Monday night still another. All through our lives God has prepared multitudes of opportunities for us to do His will and accomplish good in His name.

KEEPING THE FAITH

Paul's third idea comes out in the phrase, "I have kept the faith" (II Timothy 4:7). Paul held to the beliefs and convictions, the principles and commands of Scripture without wavering. Oh, perhaps he faltered at times. Maybe occasionally he doubted. It's possible he even thought about quitting completely. But overall, he remained true to his calling. No fleeting feelings or even serious physical pain and obstacles caused him to give up.

I recall several young men whom I discipled years ago. One of them has departed from the faith. He gave up, saying it was too hard to be a Christian. The other man continues to forge ahead. He's committed to the work of God and I see that commitment grow as the years go by.

One didn't believe. He failed to keep the faith, fight the good fight, or finish his race. There will be, if things continue as they are, no reward for him in heaven. In fact, it is questionable that he truly knows Christ. But if the other continues, he will stand before Jesus and hear those immortal words, "Well done, thou good and faithful servant."

We have to ask, is it wrong to want some reward for work well done? Not at all. It was the very thing that motivated Paul (II Timothy 4:6-8), John (III John 7), Peter (I Peter 5:2-4), James (James 1:12), and Jude (Jude 24). They wanted their lives to count for all eternity. It kept their eyes focused on whom they were serving and made all the pain worthwhile.

REWARD PERVERSIONS

Still, as wonderful as the rewards mentioned in Scripture may sound, we have to remember that the devil always seeks to twist God's truth. At times, the church has downplayed the idea of rewards so that today there is much confusion about them.

25

Have you ever heard sermons about how we will all appear before the Judgment Seat of Christ? Some say that this event will be, for some Christians, the most devastating moment of their existence. Like a giant heaven-wide broadcast, we'll witness a replay of every unrepented foul word. Every corrupt deed. Each malignant thought.

Those kinds of sermons shivered my timbers. Strange thing, though, they rarely changed my behavior. I still committed sins even though I was assured that one day everyone would see.

Another fellow told me about all the packages I'd stumble upon when I reached heaven. "What packages?" I asked. "All the prayers God wanted to answer, but which we never prayed." That was supposed to get me to pray more.

Now I look back on those messages as incomplete, potentially devastating portrayals of the character of Jesus.

THE IDEA OF AN ACCOUNTING

Some people consider the idea of heavenly rewards ludicrous, even childish. "Heaven will be the same for all of us. No one will mention the things we did on earth. We'll all be happy, without pain, full of worship. Who needs to think about such things as rewards and judgment? That's a worldly idea."

In particular, this idea of a judgment, of a time when Christ will "call us to account" for how we lived our lives in this world, is appalling to them. Some even say that such judgment runs against the very nature and character of God. "He is loving. He would never require a recounting of deeds, either bad or good."

The problem with such thinking is that it contradicts Scripture. "...For we will all stand before God's judgment seat. It is written: 'As surely as I live, says the Lord, every knee will bow before me; every tongue will confess to God.' So then, each of us will give an account of himself to God" (Romans 14:10-12). Repeatedly, God assures us we'll be "recompensed" and "rewarded" and "crowned." We will "render account" and "stand before His judgment seat."

Jesus is not a judge who plans to excoriate us for deeds undone and words unsaid; rather, He longs to commend us for what we did and the words we spoke that enlightened or encouraged. The earthly stigma we attach to the idea of a judge falls away at the realization of Jesus as our advocate, loyal friend, and royal brother.

On the other hand, if the Judgment Seat of Christ holds no fear for the Christian, what does it matter what we do now? Why sacrifice our lives for a "crown," as Paul did? Why "leave mother and father and home" in hope of receiving a hundred times that in heaven, as Jesus encouraged us in Matthew 19:29? Why even strive for holiness and godliness, confessing sin, repenting, and serving Him faithfully in the world today?

The fact is, that if there is no time of accounting, then the justice, holiness, righteousness, and goodness of God are all negated. He would not really care much how we live if He never planned to talk with us about it. Scripture emphatically declares we will all give account of our conduct as Christians. Knowing that fact should stir us with reverence as "we work out our salvation with fear and trembling, for it is God who works in you to will and to act according to his good purpose" (Philippians 2:12-13). Now that's motivation to excel for Him.

CASTES IN HEAVEN?

Another unsavory distortion of judgment and rewards is one that suggests there will somehow be classes or a hierarchy in heaven. Those who "gave it all" on earth will "have it all" up there, while others will end up with little. It's true that Scripture speaks of loss for those who failed to build properly on Christ's foundation (I Corinthians 3:12-15). It's also true that Scripture delineates many different kinds of rewards which, presumably, not all of us will obtain. (See I Corinthians 9:25; I Thessalonians 2:19-20; II Timothy 4:8; I Peter 5:4; and James 1:12.)

But more than anything else, heaven will be a place of infinite joy, love, peace, and worship. Our focus will be Christ, not what we have or don't have. While Jesus has made it plain that some "will be first" and some "will be last" (Matthew 19:30), Christ's evaluation of our service will occur without inflicting pain, hardship, shame, fear, or terror on those of us who actually are last. We will all rejoice in our place without chagrin (Revelation 21:3-4).

> *"No longer will there be any curse. The throne of God and the Lamb will be in the city, and his servants will serve him ....And they will reign for ever and ever" (Revelation 22:4-5).*

Nothing in heaven will resemble in any way what we see in the political and governmental processes on earth. Serving and leading will be perfectly melded.

WEIGHED IN THE BALANCES

The worst perversion of all is suggested in the idea that when we stand before Christ at the *bema,* He will somehow weigh our good deeds against our bad deeds and then determine whether we can even enter heaven or not. In other words, we will be saved on the basis of the goodness of our lives. Bad people go to hell. Good people make it into heaven.

Nothing could be more perverse. Salvation—the right to live with Christ for all eternity and enjoy the privileges of heaven—comes because of God's grace on the basis of our faith in Christ (Ephesians 2:8-9). The judgment of believers at Christ's *bema* has nothing to do with salvation. We gain our place in eternity based on our decision on earth to trust Christ or to reject Him. No amount of good, however sincere, can earn us a slot in heaven.

If you find yourself mystified by this, remember that we're not talking about a judgment to determine whether we're acceptable for heaven or not. We become acceptable for heaven simply by trusting Christ as Savior, Lord, and eternal Master. No person need fear that God will condemn him if he has trusted Christ for forgiveness of sins and life everlasting. If we are "in

Christ," our salvation is complete, final, and eternal. No one can take it away (John 10:28-29). Jesus Himself will welcome us to our eternal home with open arms, regardless of what our life was like here on earth. "The word is near you; it is in your mouth and in your heart, that is, the word of faith we are proclaiming: That if you confess with your mouth, Jesus is Lord, and believe in your heart that God raised him from the dead, you will be saved. For it is with your heart that you believe and are justified, and it is with your mouth that you confess and are saved" (Romans 10:8-10).

But a time of accounting for each of us is coming. We must answer to Christ for what we did with our lives as Christians. Those actions determine how we reign and rule with Christ (Revelation 5:10; II Timothy 2:11-13).

SOME TRUTH ON THE ISSUE

What, then, are the facts about the judgment seat of Christ?

First, we will all appear at Christ's judgment seat. Second Corinthians 5:10 is a primary passage. "For we must all appear before the judgment seat of Christ, that each one may receive what is due him for the things done while in the body, whether good or bad." Many other passages such as Romans 14:10-12, Romans 2:16, Matthew 16:27, and Revelation 22:12 speak of this as well. No unbeliever will stand on the victor's platform.

The "judgment seat" translates the Greek word, *bema*. The word referred to the raised platform on which a president, governor, judge, or military officer sat to address a crowd, grant awards, or render a verdict. For instance, Pilate's judgment seat before which Jesus stood at His arrest was a *bema* (Matthew 27:19). Herod Agrippa sat on a *bema* to decide an issue with several groups of citizens (Acts 12:20-23). Gallio also appeared on a *bema* when the Jews dragged Paul before him to make accusations (Acts 18:12). In each case, the judge on the *bema* listened to a case and delivered a judgment.

The other use of *bema* related to the "victor's platform."

29

Here, the winner of an athletic contest received a wreath ("crown" or *stephanos*) from the judge of the contest. Undoubtedly, this was Paul's meaning in II Corinthians 5:10 and Romans 14:10-12. If you have read *Ben Hur*, the book by Lew Wallace, you might remember the great moment when Judah ben Hur won the chariot race and received the olive-leaf crown, then turned to face the roar and acclaim of the crowd. That was a *bema* seat.

For the Christian, Scripture reveals two ideas about the *bema* of Christ: to render a verdict and to present an award.

RENDERING A VERDICT

Once a year in our business, our executive officers work long hours with a certified public accountant to determine how well our company performed that year. After they list every debit and credit, they type out the bottom line—did we make a profit or suffer a loss?

Similarly, the *bema* is, in a sense, the bottom line of our Christian lives. Four thoughts from Scripture touch on this.

1. At the **bema,** *we will answer to Jesus.* Paul says in Romans 14:12 that each one of us "will give an account of himself to God."

Two parables illuminate this accounting. In Luke 16:1-2, Jesus refers to an unjust steward who was called by his master to give an accounting of his stewardship. He was required to set the books straight and show what he'd done.

Luke 19:11-27 is even more graphic. Here, Jesus tells of three slaves who each received the same sum of money. Each slave was expected to invest that money, and when the nobleman came back, Jesus says he called in his slaves "in order to find out what they had gained with it" (Luke 19:15). Each then recounted how he'd used the master's wealth.

When we stand before the *bema* of Christ, that's precisely what we'll be doing—giving an account of how we used the gifts, abilities, opportunities, and wealth God gave us. The Lord has made a tremendous investment in each of our lives. He expects a return. The *bema* is the time of that accounting. We'll show how well, or how poorly, we utilized the things God allowed us to have in this life.

At first, the idea sounds scary. I recall two such "accountings" as a young man that make me think long and hard about the reality of standing before Jesus. The first occurred when I was a seminary student. The IRS decided to audit my grand $2000 income. I was astounded, but I gathered up my materials, went to the office, and took a seat at a desk with a cold, businesslike man sitting behind it. He peered over my returns like they were the Dead Sea Scrolls. My forehead beaded with sweat. My clothing was damp. My heart skipped with every twitch of his pointy little nose. But finally he told me, "All right. Everything is in order. Sorry to trouble you." Sorry to trouble me! More like get me ready for the nuthouse! But I said nothing, gathered up my papers and sped out—I mean a hundred yards in 9.2 seconds.

The second accounting occurred at my yearly review as a manager in a mid-sized company. I believed I'd done a good job and had even come up with a recommendation that saved us over $20,000. But I had no idea what he would say. I sidled into the office and he smiled, handed me a "report card," and asked me to read it. He'd given me high marks in many areas and I felt both relieved and happy. Then he said, "We wish to offer you a promotion and a significant raise!"

Now that's the kind of accounting I can appreciate!

While the Lord, something like that IRS examiner, might wish to scrutinize our "accounts" as His servants at the *bema,* He is far more like the happy boss about to inform us of a wonderful raise for our efforts. The *bema* is designed to crown us not club us.

2. At the bema *we'll all be examined.* Paul speaks in I Corinthians 4:4-5 of being "examined" by God. He says, "My conscience is clear, but that does not make me innocent. It is the

Lord who judges me. Therefore judge nothing before the appointed time; wait till the Lord comes. He will bring to light what is hidden in darkness and will expose the motives of men's hearts. At that time each will receive his praise from God."

The word here for "expose" literally means to "ask questions" or "examine." Pilate "examined" Jesus in Luke 23:13. Felix probed Paul in Acts 24:8. In each case, certain questions were asked and truthful answers were expected.

In this sense, not only will the Lord ask us what "business we conducted" with His gifts as in point one above, but He'll also question us about certain aspects of our work. Each of us manages certain parts of God's affairs on earth. At the *bema,* He will give us a chance to offer our own explanation. He'll probe, point out a detail, mention some missed fact, smile, listen to our answers.

But this is not a trial. At the *bema,* salvation is a closed issue. Nor is He trying to shame us. To be sure, He may mention what we could have done or should have done in some cases. Maybe He'll even bring up some sins we failed to deal with in life. But Jesus is our Advocate with the Father. He's on our side. This process illuminates His reasons for praising us, not criticizing us.

The beauty of this examination, though, is that Christ is omniscient. He will know whatever circumstances surrounded our work. He will know every variable. He'll know every trial we endured, how difficult our lot was, and what obstacles we faced. We won't be put in the position of saying, "Well, Lord, there were extenuating circumstances on that...." Or, "Lord, if you'll just let me explain!" No, we won't need to bring up any excuses. He'll know what happened with perfect knowledge. His purpose will simply be to present the truth of the situation. We'll see clearly why He rewards us for anything, and why He withholds reward on other things.

3. The **bema** *will test the quality of each Christian's work.* Merely presenting what we achieved isn't enough. The "quality" of what we did will also be proved. In I Corinthians 3:13-15, Paul tells us, "his work will be shown for what it is, because the Day will bring it to light. It will be revealed with fire, and the fire will test the quality of each man's work. If what he has built survives, he will receive his reward. If it is burned up, he will suffer loss; he himself will be saved, but only as one escaping through the flames."

At the *bema,* Christ will pass the sum total of our lives through a spiritual fire. Some parts will survive the heat of the divine inferno. Other elements will be burned up. The process of purifying silver illustrates this idea. The smith heats the silver until it melts. Once liquified, any light impurities float to the surface, while heavier ones slide to the bottom. In the middle the smith finds the purest silver.

In some ways, our lives are like a lode of silver dug from a mine. Dirt, other metals, and rock all clot around and through the chunk. Putting it through the fire separates the real silver from the refuse.

This fire tests the quality of the Christian's life whether it's "good or bad" (II Corinthians 5:10). That is, Christ is not examining the moral quality of our work, but the eternal, lasting quality. *"For we must all appear before the judgment seat of Christ, that each one may receive what is due him for the things done while in the body, whether good or bad."* The word here for "bad" is *phaulos* which relates to the worth of something. Some works are worthless in terms of God's kingdom and eternity. Others have great value. The fire will test whether a work lasts or not.

HOW?

How will this take place? Will there be a literal fire? How can one subject "love" to a fire? Or a word of thanks? Or a prayer? Or a good deed? All these things are abstractions, not concrete bits of wood, hay, and straw.

The key here is what fire does. It burns up anything not made of the right materials. Worthless, selfish, or hypocritical things—wood, hay, and straw—go up in smoke. But gold and silver only become finer.

At the *bema* our lives will go through a divine fire that determines the eternal value of all we achieved. Somehow this fire will consume anything not in line with God's glory, but it will refine anything that was right on target.

Suppose a man gives a child a cup of cold water, knowing what Jesus said in Matthew 10:42 about such deeds. He expects that Jesus will give him some special reward for this deed. From our perspective, the deed looks perfect.

But at the *bema,* this deed is placed under the magnifying glass of heaven. The fire heats up, and we begin to go inside the man and see all that really happened. We may discover that he gave the child a drink to shut him up. The child was screaming about being thirsty, the man couldn't stand it any longer, and he finally got up and handed him the cup. But inside the man grumbled at the inconvenience. None of this may have been evident at the time. The man could easily mask his real feelings and serve up the cup with real verve. But in the fire of truth, when all the facts are revealed, we see that it was a worthless deed. It gets burned up because the motives were all out of kilter.

On the other hand, we find another man working in Bangladesh during a terrible famine. He gives a child a cup of cold water, but he has no smile on his face. In fact he's grimacing. At the time, the child thinks this man quite nasty.

But the light of Christ's fire exposes the truth. This man was suffering from merciless back pain. He grimaced from that pain, not because he didn't want to help the child. He longed only to please God and do what was right. He was not thinking of rewards, but in the light of eternity that deed could last.

In this sense, our whole lives will be subjected to Christ's fire. Whatever has lasting value will only grow purer.

4. *Before the* bema, *our works will become evident to all.*

I find this fourth element in the words of II Corinthians 5:10 where Paul says we must all "appear" before the judgment seat of Christ. The word "appear" means to "make manifest, to become plain, evident, clear." The same word is used in I Corinthians 3:13 where Paul says each man's work "will be shown for what it is."

This judgment will take place in public, just as the Roman *bema* was public. Our deeds will, in light of the accounting, examination, and testing, become plain to all. Everyone will see the justice of Christ's decision. No one will ever dispute, through all eternity, that He was wrong.

That's a rather scary idea.

Several years ago, I appeared in traffic court because I forgot to register my car in time to change my license plate. I remember the motley crew that preceded me. People arrested for drunken driving stood and gave some truly incredible explanations for their behavior. "I had to get home because my dog had to be fed and I forgot until I reached the bar." "I was only drinking beer. That doesn't have that much alcohol in it."

Then there were people who ran red lights, drove over the speed limit, or failed to stop at stop signs. One man said, "I couldn't have been driving that fast because my tires are worn down." The whole court snickered as they heard some of these stories.

I remember having to walk up before that judge in front of all those people to offer my explanation. I envisioned someone standing and crying, "Yeah, sure, Littleton!" And, "Tell me another one!"

Our earthly ideas of standing before a judge can certainly corrupt what we might think will happen in heaven. We won't stand at the *bema* to make a defense at all. And no one will be looking for a good snicker. While we must approach the idea with absolute sobriety and integrity, the Lord also wants us to come full of hope and joy. This is a victor's platform, not a victim's garrote.

Our Lord is saying to us, "Take note. What you do today and every day matters. One day you will give an account to Me in public and all will see and agree with My verdict." That truth rebukes any life of indifferent ease, but it also reinforces any Christian who pursues service and righteousness with a Christlike spirit.

A RECOMPENSE

That brings us to the second element of the *bema*. Once everything has been weighed and tested, there's a reward. To the victor goes a wreath. To the Christian goes a crown—and much more.

We look again at the words of II Corinthians 5:10. Paul says that each of us will be given "his due" or "recompensed" for his deeds in the body. The word for "recompensed" means to "receive back." It's a repayment. You do such and such work; you get a wage, a reward. Jesus says that that spiritual reward may be hundreds of times more valuable than what you did initially, but that's the way God pays (Matthew 19:29-30).

It's important to realize what Paul means by the phrase "according to what he did, whether good or bad" (II Corinthians 5:10). The idea behind "what he did" is a summary, a totality. Paul means that our whole lives will be weighed, not just single acts. We won't be receiving a crown or jewel for each deed; rather, Christ will judge the character and conduct of our lives as a whole. We'll be rewarded on the basis of the total effort, in the same way that many organizations give people "lifetime achievement" awards.

This truth offers hope to all of us no matter where we are in our Christian lives. We can always start now. No matter how little we've done up to now, or how insignificant our lives look, we can always look forward to the fact that our whole lives will be considered before any reward is given. It's a total accounting, a bottom line situation.

One of my employees made a tremendous mistake one year

which required writing him up. Fortunately, he'd also done plenty of things right. When we had his yearly review, I pulled out his file and went through the things I had in it. I decided to recommend him for a raise and a change in title.

As he listened, his face suddenly took on a deeply concerned expression. He said, "But what about...?" And he asked me about the infraction. I showed him my review. There was no mention of it. Also, I pulled the write-up out of the file and handed it to him. "You can have it," I said. "It's out of the file. It'll never be in there again."

One thing we need to remember at the *bema* is that all those "write-ups" from the past—our sins—will never be brought up. Jesus has placed them as far as the east is from the west. They're in the depths of the sea. The *bema* is meant to be a moment of victory, a sign that we won, not a reminder of previous losses.

SOME STARK THOUGHTS

Many Christians may read these words and weep. "What has my life counted for?" they moan. For them, they believe the *bema* will be a badge of shame.

If that is what you're thinking, the rest of this book will be a great encouragement. The Scriptures speak of many mundane and "insignificant" things that count in the eyes of God. Anyone who sincerely plods forward for Jesus in whatever capacity has much to anticipate. No one has to equal Billy Graham or Corrie ten Boom in order to gain the same rewards in heaven. Christ said "many who are first will be last, and many who are last will be first." He looks at our lives in terms of what He endowed us with, and how we used the endowment. There's no comparison to anyone else. God may simply have given others more to use.

At the same time, these truths come as a stark warning to Christians who frivol away their lives, time, and money in pursuit of personal pleasure and ease. God has stern words for those who waste or abuse His primary resources—us and those around us. We cannot sashay through life planning to "start tomorrow" or next week. We cannot neglect truth, righteousness, and holy conduct now and think we'll whip up to the *bema* and carry away all the honors. One day each of us will have his moment before Christ. We'll look into those eyes that see from eternity through each microsecond of our lives and the truth will be all too evident.

Let me offer some stark thoughts in this matter that we should weigh solemnly as we get up each morning.

First, realize that your life counts for something now—either loss or gain, for all eternity. Now is the only time we can serve Christ in this body. Now is the only moment we can do good. Each moment affects eternity. Now is the only time we can lead another to Christ.

We cannot discount that principle. When we stand alone before Jesus, we won't be able to blame anyone else. He requires that we answer for what we did with what He gave us.

That's a sobering thought. It makes me realize that I can't waste time, blow my money, horde my possessions, squander opportunities. Everything counts.

Second, take a hard look at your life in the light of these facts. What are we doing with our time, our money, our gifts? One day the fact that we knew the television schedule may be a mark of abomination to our hearts. We may reel in horror as we see how we frittered our lives away in foolishness. It will all come out. We can't escape it. We are accountable for all we have done.

Third, these truths should help us live in great fear of God. "Fearing" God is not something I think about a lot. But as I've grown as a Christian, I've developed some genuine fear along the way. Fear of committing sin. Fear of displeasing Him. Fear of Him coming back and not finding me serving Him.

That's not to say I walk about with a long face, shrinking in terror from every shadow that crosses my path. But a healthy dose of the fear of God is something we all often need. The book of Proverbs says a lot to us about fearing the Lord. It is the beginning of wisdom (1:7), adds length to life (10:27), brings health (3:7-8), gives a secure fortress (14:26), and is a fountain of life (14:27).

Fourth, these truths ought to give us great hope. It challenges me to realize that nothing will be overlooked. No deed, however small, will be forgotten by the Lord. Everything we do weighs in the balances of eternity.

That drives me. It doesn't mater if no one notices. What matters is that *He* notices.

Allan C. Emery writes in his book, *A Turtle on a Fencepost*, how a porter once spoke with his father on a train trip from St. Louis to Boston. They shared their mutual faith. Mr. Emery noticed a certain hesitation and fear in the porter's eyes, but he wasn't sure what it was. The man said nothing about it at first, but at the end of the trip, he came to Mr. Emery, saying, "Do you suppose I could ask you a question after my passengers leave?"

When he finished with the others, he told the story of how his godly mother instilled in all her children the value of a good education. He longed to go to college and become a preacher. He had taken a job with the railroad as a waiter to save money for his schooling. However, his younger brother went in a different direction, drinking and partying and living for the devil. At the same time he was accepted at a college, his younger brother was marvelously converted and felt a call to the ministry. At his brother's request, he offered to continue working on the railroad to pay his college expenses and then go after his brother finished.

But it was not to be. The younger brother finished school and went on to become a nationally known preacher who led thousands to Christ. But the porter never did. He told Mr. Emery with tears in his eyes, "I'm too old now to go." It was obvious he felt he'd failed—his mother, himself, and his Lord.

Then he said, "Mr. Emery, my question is this: Do you suppose the Lord will give me some credit for the souls my brother led to Him?"

Mr. Emery's heart nearly turned over with compassion for this pained man, but he had a ready answer from I Samuel 30:24: "The share of the man who stayed with the supplies is to be the same as that of him who went down to the battle. All will share alike."

I wonder sometimes if that story is not the story of each of us. Many of us have helped and supported others who went on to do great deeds, but when we look at our own lives, we see little of note.

Nonetheless, God sees what we don't see. His ledger books are far different from ours. I suspect that there will be many at His judgment seat who take away rewards they can't even imagine. The last will be first. All the little people in little places doing little things will find themselves in the first ranks of heaven.

Nothing—NOTHING!—is small in God's eyes. It all counts.

-3-
What Kinds of Rewards?

One day a panhandler came to John D. Rockefeller, telling him, "I traveled thirty miles down here just to meet you, and everybody I met assured me you were the most generous man in New York."

Rockefeller, a billionaire at the time, asked, "Are you going back by the same route?"

"Probably," said the panhandler.

"In that case you can do me a great favor," said Rockefeller. "Deny the rumor."

Rumor has it that God Almighty is the most generous Being in the universe. But He never says, "Deny it!" Rather, He wants us to shout from the mountaintops: "I want to make your cup overflow! I want to fill your eternity with every good thing. Follow My Son and I will pile it on." Giving rewards for work well done is not a capitalist idea; it's straight from the heart of God. He assures us, "I will recompense every believer according to what he has done, whether good or bad."

God promises marvelous rewards once we reach heaven. We will not reap them in this world. No matter how much some might like to proclaim a gospel of health, wealth, and prosperity, that is the rumor that must be denied. God reserves the true riches for His eternal kingdom.

Yet, not only does God promise to reward us for work well

done, He also insists that there are different levels of reward. Some will receive more than others. In this regard, Jesus told two parables.

One was about the laborers in the vineyard (Matthew 20:1-16). All the laborers, regardless of the amount of work they did, received one day's pay for his work. The fellows who worked eight hours received the same amount as those who worked one hour.

This is a glorious illustration of the gift of salvation. Everyone receives eternal life regardless of how long they served the Lord. Both the girl who becomes a Christian at five-years-old and serves the Lord faithfully for eighty years, and the thief on the cross who believed at the last moment of earthly life will receive eternal life and fellowship forever in heaven.

But the second parable was the story of the talents (Matthew 25:14-30). Here, each individual received a certain amount of money—one five talents, another two talents, and a third received one talent. Each was to invest the money to make more money. When the judgment came, they presented what they had to the king. But each received a different reward. Why?

The purpose of this parable was to illustrate how God rewards us in light of the abilities, strengths, and wisdom He's given us. If we have tremendous gifts but use them poorly, we'll receive only a small reward or maybe none at all. But if we have only slight abilities, yet use them to great result, we'll receive a great reward.

That's part of the purpose of rewards. Some rewards are really gifts and come as a result of believing in Christ. Everyone gets them. Other rewards are specific returns for work rendered for Christ.

GIFTS

Scripture speaks of a number of such "gifts" that we all receive by virtue of our faith in Christ. These are not rewards. A reward is extra, a payment, a wage, a recompense.

Gifts come because of God's grace. We do nothing to obtain them except believe. Faith in Christ and repentance from sin are not works in God's eyes. They are acts of obedience on the basis of His command, and the vicarious atonement of His Son. They are the conditions of salvation. And because of our faith, God has chosen to shower upon us a number of priceless gifts and honors.

Suppose a man—let's call him Tom—gave his friend, Harry, a brand new Porsche 944. It was a gift out of a heart of love and grace.

But imagine that Harry said, "I really appreciate this, Tom. But I'd like to do something in return for it. What can I do?"

Tom assures him there's nothing he can or should do. It's a gift.

Nonetheless, Harry presses on: "No, I really want to do something. How about if I shine your shoes for three days straight?"

Tom doesn't really like it, but he says, "All right. Go ahead."

So Harry shines Tom's shoes for three days. Afterward, Harry can say, "Tom gave me this car for three shoeshines."

Preposterous? Of course. Who would give someone a Porsche for three shoeshines?

In the same way, how could God give us eternal life, heaven, and all the other good gifts of His grace—for any number of works we might do in this lifetime? Truly, "God doesn't give eternal life for shoeshines!"

Only faith can lay hold of such gifts. Then what gifts accompany our salvation in Christ? When we accept Christ, God not only gives us salvation—complete pardon from having to pay the penalty for our sins—but also the prospect of:

•Heaven/eternal life—John 3:16, 5:24, 10:27-29.

•A spiritual, imperishable, glorious body—I Corinthians 15:42-44.

•Eternal fellowship with Christ—John 14:1-3.

•A place in God's house—John 14:1-3; Revelation 21:3-4.

- An inheritance—Ephesians 1:18-19; Colossians 3:22-24.
- An end to pain and suffering—Revelation 22:3, 7:16-17, 21:4.
- The privilege of seeing God's face—Revelation 22:4.
- The privilege of reigning with Him forever—Revelation 22:5.
- The privilege of participating in the judgment of evil angels and evil people—I Corinthians 6:2-3.
- Being part of God's family, sons and daughters—Romans 8:14-17; Revelation 21:7.
- Sharing God's glory—Romans 8:17.

Review that list several times. If you are a Christian, God intends to give you all those gifts simply because you believed and followed Jesus Christ. We can do nothing to earn any of it. We obtain it all only by faith.

Why does God offer us so much? For one reason: because He wants to. He loves to make our cups run over.

REWARDS

Clearly, though, there are other rewards God gives which can only be called recompense for services rendered. The Bible speaks of rewards that relate to personal activity in this world. I see several categories.

CROWNS

When Scripture says we'll wear crowns, it speaks of two elements of our salvation: we have won a great victory, and, also, we are the Savior's personal V.I.P.s.

The Bible speaks of several crowns:

- *The crown of life* (James 1:12, Revelation 2:10). Both James and John indicate that those who endure through harsh earthly trials and keep the faith will wear this crown. Christians who persevere through persecution certainly qualify, but James indicates that any trial in which our faith in God is challenged—and through which we persevere—deserves this crown.

44

• *The crown of righteousness* (II Timothy 4:8). Paul spoke of how he "fought the good fight, finished the course, and kept the faith." He longed for the Lord Jesus to come and looked forward to being crowned personally by Him.

• *The imperishable crown* (I Corinthians 9:24-27). It's not clear if this is a separate category, but Paul mentions it as the crown that those who have run a disciplined, honest, and purposeful race will win.

• *The crown of glory* (I Peter 5:4). Christ gives this crown to those who lead, guide, and govern well. It may not be strictly reserved for elders and leaders, but the Bible refers to it only once in the context of elders and overseers.

• *The crown of rejoicing* (Philippians 4:1, I Thessalonians 2:17-18). Again, it's unclear whether this is a separate crown or simply a metaphor Paul uses for the joy he will experience in seeing those he's led to Christ in heaven. But if that is so, then anyone who led others to the Lord and discipled them will wear this crown of rejoicing and exultation.

Scripture doesn't clarify precisely what these crowns are—whether they are actual crowns worn on the head or something else. However, whatever they are, we won't keep them. We'll cast them at Christ's feet in recognition of His glory as it says in Revelation 4:10. Those crowns point not so much to what we have done, but to what Christ did in us.

Paul says in I Corinthians 4:7, "For who makes you different from anyone else? What do you have that you did not receive? And if you did receive it, why do you boast as though you did not?" Our lives, our deeds, all our efforts are nothing less than gifts from Him to us. He worked them in us...for His glory. Jesus said in John 15:5, "Apart from me you can do nothing."

We cannot accomplish anything of lasting value without His complete and unwavering grace to us. Those crowns point to Him, to His goodness, His mercy, and His love. When we wear them in the assembly of the righteous—if we wear them at all—they do not point to the one wearing them, but to Him who awarded it. He planned and executed whatever good we accomplished. A crown doesn't give us reason for boasting in what we did, but what Christ did through us from beginning to end. Because of that, we cast them in reverence and praise at His feet.

PLACES OF AUTHORITY

The Bible also speaks of positions of authority that some receive as a reward for their faithfulness on earth. This involves...

•The right to rule and lead others (Matthew 25:23). They gain this place because of their faithfulness in serving and managing God's people, gifts, and resources while on earth.

•Authority in the new kingdom (Revelation 2:26). Those who recognize false teaching and do Christ's will gain the right to lead and administrate in the new kingdom.

•The right to reign with Christ (II Timothy 2:12). Christ gives this to those who endure through the temptations and difficulties of life with their faith and commitment to Him intact.

PERSONAL PRAISE FROM JESUS

Several passages of Scripture speak of the personal recognition and praise that Jesus Himself will utter on our behalf. Many are familiar with Matthew 25:23, where the master says to his servant, "Well done, good and faithful servant." This servant used his master's gifts skillfully and faithfully. In the end, he was rewarded with a personal accolade.

First Corinthians 4:5 also speaks of the "praise from God" that Christians acquire for faithfulness and right motives. While eternity will be a time of perfect worship, love, and praise of Jesus, He also has chosen to take a moment to praise each of us for how we conducted our lives.

Some may think, "Why should God praise us?" Indeed! Why should He? There is no reason except that He is gracious and He wants us to look forward to it. Otherwise, why would He reveal it in Scripture? Ultimately, we can do nothing to deserve that praise. Like the unprofitable servant in Luke 17:9-10, why should God thank us for doing what we were commanded to do? Even if we somehow managed to live perfect lives of faith, service, love, and gratitude after our conversion, we could do little more than say, "I have only done what you commanded, no more." And He could understandably answer, "That's correct. All you are is an unworthy servant. You've only done what you should have done!"

Our Lord, however, has chosen not to treat us as slaves, but as friends, as sons and daughters, like members of His royal family (John 15:9-15). In His grace, He has decided to praise us for deeds which He through His Spirit worked in us. He, in His gracious bounty to us, wants to reward us for acts of goodness which we would never have done except that He motivated, guided, empowered, and encouraged us every step of the way!

The *bema* will be the greatest of all eulogies, one that will never be forgotten, one that could never be equated on earth. Yet, it will all reflect back in praise to God. If we feel anything, it will be nothing less than a desire to praise and love Him all the more.

Most of all, we must refuse to think of it in worldly terms. It will not be something designed to get us to compare one to the other. "How many words did He say about you?" "You know, Joe D. over there got five minutes more than any of us!" There's nothing in all of our experience that can prepare us for what will happen when Christ offers praise on our behalf. How it will happen is inexplicable. Yet, the result will be greater and deeper worship of Him.

EXALTATION IN THE EYES OF CREATION

James 4:10 reminds us, "Humble yourselves before the Lord, and He will lift you up." First Peter 5:6 says, "Humble yourselves, therefore, under God's mighty hand, that He may lift you up in due time." Matthew 5:3 reminds us, "Blessed are the poor in spirit, for theirs is the kingdom of heaven."

47

Were you ever the last one chosen in gym class for the team? Were you ever the one given away (not traded) on the Little League team? Do you ever feel as though nothing you've ever done really matters? That desire for earthly recognition eats at some, but we don't have to worry about our unhonored contributions to God's kingdom.

When we arrive in heaven, Jesus Himself will claim us as His personal friends. He will acknowledge us before the Father and His angels (Revelation 3:5). We won't be the ones left out, the people who slipped through the cracks, or those who simply don't cut it with the rest of the stars. No, at that moment, we will be revered friends and family of the Creator of the Universe.

AN "ETERNAL WEIGHT OF GLORY"

Second Corinthians 4:17-18 speaks of another reward, the "weight of glory." The verse reads, "For our light and momentary troubles are achieving for us an eternal glory that far outweighs them all. So we fix our eyes not on what is seen, but on what is unseen." "Glory" refers to one's importance and prestige in the eyes of others. God's glory is often spoken of in terms of light. That "God is glorious" refers to His infinite majesty. No one compares to Him.

In this sense, Jesus has chosen to give us a taste of that same glory. Perhaps we'll reflect His own perfection to all of creation in special and marvelous ways that only God understands.

I don't know—nor does anyone else—precisely how these things will all be carried out. But it's clear God intends to pour these rewards on us in tidal waves. His children, His people, will be the pride and joy of all of His creation. And each of us will point to Jesus Himself, our Lord and Master.

SOME SPECIAL GIFTS

Scripture also speaks of a number of strange and intriguing rewards that are named but not defined. They are such things as:
• A special right to eat of the tree of life (Revelation 2:7). This

is for those who overcome false teaching and hardships.

•Not being hurt by the second death (Revelation 2:11)—for those who overcome persecution.

•Partaking of the hidden manna (Revelation 2:17)—for not holding false teaching and for remaining faithful.

•Receiving the white stone (Revelation 2:17)—for not holding false teaching.

•Receiving the morning star (Revelation 2:28)—for doing God's will.

•Being clothed in white garments (Revelation 3:5)—for keeping the truth and overcoming.

•Having Christ confess our name before the Father and the angels (Revelation 3:5)—for obeying, repenting, and keeping the truth.

•Being made a pillar in God's temple (Revelation 3:12)—for doing right and enduring patiently.

•Having the name of God written on us (Revelation 3:12)—for doing right and not denying the Lord.

•The right to sit with Christ on His throne (Revelation 3:21)—for enduring God's discipline and repenting.

These rewards sound fascinating. Some appear simple—like reigning with Christ—but we can't fully appreciate their meaning now. Others offer an intriguing glimpse of the largess of God. He is the Philanthropist *par excellence*, the Bright and Abounding Benevolence. Like He says in Ephesians 2:7, He wants to show us "the incomparable riches of His grace, expressed in his kindness to us in Christ Jesus."

A SOBERING THOUGHT

As we conclude, I think we need to remember a sobering truth about these rewards: God doesn't have to offer us a single reward or accolade for anything we have done. He owes us nothing. Even if we lived perfect lives unmarred by a single pinpoint of sin, we'd remain in His debt. All we could say was that we did only what we were supposed to do.

But God is no tyrant, demanding a master/slave relationship. Instead, He offers us the privilege of princeship. He calls us to a life of integrity and holiness, and He promises to make it worth all the trouble. He gives us eternal life simply for believing His Son is His Son and accepting the sacrifice of His blood as the covering for our sin.

So why is God doing this? Why is He offering us so much for so little? We'll look at part of the answer in the next chapter.

-4-
Why Does God Offer Us Rewards?

Why does God plan to reward us? What's His purpose in giving rewards?

In one sense it appears a contradiction. Salvation is a gift. People are saved by faith alone, not good deeds. Why? So no man could boast that he'd earned heaven on his own (Ephesians 2:8-9). So how can our good deeds enter into it if God has made it clear that it's all by grace?

Imagine a king has two subjects who are brothers. They both become criminals—stealing, robbing, lying, murdering. But one day they both learn that the king has invited everyone to become princes in his house. He will forgive all their crimes if they'd just come.

The first brother rejects the proposition. He says, "It's a trick. I don't believe it. Anyway, I like my work the way it is. There's no point in becoming a prince."

One day he is captured and brought before the king forcibly. He admits nothing, spits in the king's face, rejects the king, his kingdom, and his gifts. The king says, "Your will be done." He sentences the man to life imprisonment in the dungeon. Justice was done.

The second brother, however, believes the king's invitation and decides there might be something to this prince business. He goes to the king's castle, admits his crimes, and receives forgiveness. The king makes him a prince.

For awhile, this prince lolls about the palace, enjoying the riches of the king. But soon he wonders what a prince is supposed to do. So he asks, "What now?" The king sends him out into the world to do good deeds and to help people everywhere he can, in any way he can. "After everything is done," the king says, "I'll reward you with special kingly rewards."

This astounds him since he's already received so much, but he likes the idea of pleasing the king and goes out, performing good deeds, sharing, and loving the king's people. Finally, there comes the day of reckoning. All the princes line up before the king. They give an account of all their travels and deeds. At the end, the king gives each a special reward. The second brother never has to pay anything for his crimes because he was forgiven.

So it is with God because we are forgiven in Christ. He's perfectly just and He will render perfect justice on our behalf—with a twist. It's not just that God rewards us for a job well done. But God, because He is gracious and generous, enjoys going far beyond anything we might anticipate. He gives us justice with a cherry on top. Or should I say, a whole cherry tree! Better yet, a whole universe of cherry trees and every other good thing.

REASONS FOR REWARDS

What then is the divine reasoning behind rewards? Why does God offer them to us?

1. To motivate us to do good.

In this world people are often tempted to say, "What use is it to serve God? Both good and bad people die. Frequently, bad people have an easier time than good people. It doesn't pay to serve God." Job made this remark during his time of illness (Job 21:1-16). Psalm 73:1-14 records a similar outlook. It sometimes appears that the efforts of the saints go overlooked, while worldly, godless people drag away the greatest rewards this world has to offer.

But Psalm 73:17 shows us where our true perspective originates: "Till I entered the sanctuary of God; then I understood their final destiny." Our payday is not in this world. Galatians 6:9 reminds us, "Let us not become weary in doing good, for at the proper time we will reap a harvest if we do not give up." God has set a time when each good work will be recompensed. Sometimes God rewards us in this world. If we work hard, we'll see some tangible results. But, ultimately, nothing in this world can equal what will happen in heaven.

We must move away from our worldly, American mentality. The 1960s through the 1980s were an unprecedented time of economic growth and prosperity for the United States, while most of the world teetered on the edge of poverty. Economically, Americans live in the top ten percent of all those on earth. But it's a powerful deception. We think we have the good life now, but the Bible offers us the truth. Loving this world is foolish; it will all pass away (James 1:10-11).

As we reconcile ourselves with the truth of heaven's rewards, Paul's words to the Corinthians encourage us: "Therefore, my dear brothers, stand firm. Let nothing move you. Always give yourselves fully to the work of the Lord, because you know that your labor in the Lord is not in vain" (I Corinthians 15:58).

Notice the words, "in vain." Even though we may not reap an immediate payment for our efforts in the here and now, God says, "Don't worry. Be steadfast. Don't let anyone dislodge you from your conviction. Anything done for Me will be rewarded. I forget nothing."

It's too easy in the roar of the Battle of Life to let Satan drown out the truths of Scripture. We throw down our armor and shout, "What's the use? Nobody cares about what I'm doing." But Jesus said, "If anyone gives even a cup of cold water to one of these little ones because he is my disciple, I tell you the truth, he will certainly not lose his reward" (Matthew 10:42). That

Scripture almost makes me want to go into the water fountain business for elementary schools! God urges us to stay in the battle by assuring us, "My payday is coming. Hang tough."

2. To get us to put our eyes on heaven.

A second reason God gives rewards is to get us to put our eyes on heaven, not on the things of this world. Jesus gave us a marvelous truth in Matthew 6:19. He told us not to lay up "treasures on earth" but to store up "treasures in heaven."

Earthly treasures lose value, get stolen, rust out, get eaten away. But heavenly treasures only accrue in value. When our eyes are on the things waiting for us in heaven, we can forget what's down here. "For where your treasure is, there your heart will be also" (Matthew 6:21).

Paul said it another way in Colossians 3:2: "Set your minds on things above, not on earthly things." Consider several principles in the Word against those in the world.

THE WORLD SAYS	GOD SAYS
1. Winning is everything.	1. "Run in such a way that you may win."
2. Be number one.	2. "Seek first His kingdom."
3. Watch out for number one.	3. "Serve one another."
4. An eye for an eye.	4. "Do not resist him who is evil."
5. Get money, as much as you can.	5. "The love of money is the root of all evil."
6. Do what you have to do.	6. "Do not grow weary of doing good."
7. Seek pleasure.	7. "Endure hardship."

8. Go for the gusto.	8. "Please Him in all respects."
9. All truth is relative.	9. "Thy word is truth."
10. There are no absolutes.	10. "I am the way, the truth and the life."

If we set our minds on column one, we'll behave one way, if on column two, an entirely different way.

3. To motivate us to purify ourselves.

A third reason for rewards is to motivate us to purify ourselves. John said, "...We know that when he appears, we shall be like him, for we shall see him as he is. Everyone who has this hope in him purifies himself, just as he is pure" (I John 3:2-3).

John meant that the moment Jesus returns and we look on His face, we shall be like Him in body and spirit. This should motivate us to purify ourselves so "that we may be confident and unashamed before him at His coming" (I John 2:28).

One time when my wife was away, I was reading a book in our family room. My daughter had ravaged it the night before, and I hadn't made her clean up the mess because I felt too tired to help her. That afternoon, she came down the stairs and cried, "Daddy, Mrs. Everett (a neighbor) needs your help. She can't get into her house." And suddenly, there stood Mrs. Everett, grinning and standing right in the middle of the debris. It startled me how the condition of the room suddenly took on a new light with a stranger viewing it.

Needless to say, I cleaned up the mess that night. Later on, I wondered how I might have felt had that person been Jesus. I was embarrassed in the presence of another human. But what about God? Knowing Christ is coming back to call us to account inspires purity. We don't want to face Him in shame, knowing that He may have nothing good to say to us...having found our lives in complete disorder.

4. To encourage us to persevere.

The reality of rewards should also encourage us to persevere. Jesus reminds us in Matthew 5:12, "Rejoice and be glad, because great is your reward in heaven, for in the same way they persecuted the prophets who were before you." Knowing that there's a payday—even if it's not in this world—can supercharge a Christian in the face of persecution, problems, trials, and afflictions.

All of us struggle with the problem of obeying Christ in the daily grind of life. If the big knocks don't deck us, it's the little nudges, irritations, and difficulties. It's so easy to think, "God won't notice if I slack off." Or, "It's such a little thing."

But knowing He's taking notes for even miniscule words and deeds should encourage us to endure—and to change. What did Paul think as he slogged through city after city, receiving nothing but beatings, cursing, disputes, and hatred? He fixed his eyes on one thing. He said, "I press on toward the goal to win the prize for which God has called me heavenward in Christ Jesus" (Philippians 3:14). Paul's eyes were not on his troubles, but on Christ and His promise of rewards. As the apostle goes on to say, "All of us who are mature should take such a view of things" (3:15).

One evening while I was writing this book, my wife called from her mother's house to say she couldn't latch a new window and felt afraid. She asked me—after a long, grueling day in which I'd been up until 3 a.m. the night before—to come over and fix it. I grumbled, but she knew I was writing this book and she said, "I'm sure the Lord will reward you."

Ah, the wiles of a woman! But it did make me laugh. And you know, it's uncanny, but as I drove over and then back, I sensed a pleasure—perhaps His pleasure—in doing something to help another—especially someone I had pledged to love as Christ loves the church. There's real peace, joy, and just plain pleasure in doing good. He's made us that way.

5. To keep us faithful to the Word.

If I know that my performance in certain arenas in my job determines whether or not I receive a raise or promotion, I tend to give priority to that area. God understands that mentality. That's why He tells us, "Watch out that you do not lose what you have worked for, but that you may be rewarded fully" (II John 8).

It is possible to lose rewards. Paul tells us in I Corinthians 3 that some works will burn up and the Christian will suffer loss. Similarly, certain rewards may be given or withheld pending our faithfulness to doctrine and the truths of Scripture. Realizing that I could lose heavenly rewards because I gave my money, time, or effort to causes that obscure the gospel of Christ drives me to investigate those whom I support. Christians cannot glibly give to just anyone, saying, "It all goes for the same cause."

It doesn't. There are multitudes of charlatans, deceivers, and false teachers out there taking the time and resources of Christians. Those Christians may be in for a monstrous surprise when they reach Christ's judgment seat. They might find that everything they labored for is burned to ashes.

6. To encourage us to build qualitatively on the foundation.

By way of contrast to the above principle, we see that God wants us to build qualitatively on the foundation of Christ. "If any man builds on this foundation using gold, silver, costly stones, wood, hay, or straw, his work will be shown for what it is, because the Day will bring it to light. It will be revealed with fire, and the fire will test the quality of each man's work" (I Corinthians 3:12-13).

We all need to take a hard look at what we're doing for Christ We may find that we've added nothing to the foundation but weak, worthless, perishable items. Paul says it's possible to build on the foundation of Christ with the wrong materials.

I often think of the widow's mites in this regard. Jesus sat by the treasury watching people put in their gifts. The Pharisees unloaded vast amounts of gold and silver. Then along came this widow with two farthings (one-quarter of a penny each). As she dropped them in Jesus said, "...Truly I say to you, this poor widow put in more than all the contributors to the treasury; for they all put in out of their surplus, but she, out of her poverty, put in all she owned, all she had to live on" (Mark 12:43-44, NASB).

Suppose we could see as God sees. In the divine accounting, it's possible that we might have this conversation.

"So what happened with the money that all the rich folks put in?"

"It was used in building the Temple, adding rooms, that kind of thing."

"What happened to the Temple?"

"It was destroyed in 70 A.D. Not one stone was left upon the other."

"And that's all the reward they got?"

"Yes."

"Then what about the widow's mites? How were they accounted for?"

"The two farthings were credited against a certain scribe's work. Specifically, it paid for his time in copying Isaiah 53."

"That doesn't sound so magnificent."

"Oh? For your information that particular manuscript was used for many years in the Temple, was read from by many of the apostles, and even used in Paul's arguments against the Pharisees. Several thousand conversions occurred through people who preached and read from this text and manuscript."

"Hmmm. So the widow will receive rewards in heaven for all those conversions?"

"Absolutely."

"That's rather amazing."

"Hey, that's only the beginning. The manuscript itself went on to become the standard on which many other manuscripts were based, and so it lasted through the ages with multitudes coming to Christ through hearing the passage read and explained."

"You mean she'll receive more rewards for this kind of thing?"

"Right. But that's not all. There's also the story about the widow in Scripture. Thousands of believers have been touched and inspired by her example."

"You mean she'll also receive rewards for that?"

"Of course. Everything will be perfectly accounted for. Every effect. Every result."

"This is quite astounding. Anything else?"

"Yes, there's the influence of the widow on her contemporaries, her life before and after the gift. Many of those effects still go on until now."

"You've got to be kidding. All that on two farthings?'

"Oh, there's much more. For instance, there was the impact upon the angels as they witnessed it....There are the multitudes of sermons and messages through the ages based on this story....There is...."

"Stop. Stop. This is too much. Is this what happens with all believers?"

"Certainly. It will all come out in the end."

I don't know about you, but such ideas inspire me. Knowing that every deed, however small in the eyes of the world, will be shone in the light of heaven for the true value Christ placed on it should give us great encouragement. Sacrifices like that of the widow win Christ's praise, even if the world sneers at them. One day, Christ's praise will be the only praise that matters.

7. To force us to take note of our motives.

One area we often neglect is that of motives. The Scriptures remind us that motives rank high in importance. Paul says in Romans 2:16 that God will "judge men's secrets through Christ Jesus."

The word here for "secrets" means what is "concealed,

hidden, not brought out into the light." This includes not only the secret things people do in dark alleys, the quiet of their homes, and elsewhere, but also the secret words and thoughts that live in our hearts. Paul encouraged the Corinthians not to pass judgment on people's work for Christ until Jesus came, because *He* would reveal their true motives (I Corinthians 4:5).

In God's reward system, motives are paramount. We cannot do anything for show and fool Him. The Pharisees "sounded a trumpet" when they gave alms. They prayed on street corners in order to be seen by men. They neglected their appearance so people would honor them for fasting. But Jesus derided their motives. He knew they were faking it; that they weren't sacrificing anything for Him. Because they did it only for worldly acclaim, that was all the reward they'd ever get. Christians need to examine their motives. We need to be acutely aware of and resist the pride, envy, greed, and jealousy that permeates so many of our actions. Only through admitting and confessing these ungodly motives can we free ourselves from them and reach any semblance of purity of heart.

8. To give everyone an equal chance at great rewards.

Our world boils over with inequities. Why was I born into a stable, middle class family, given a college education, and offered so many good things in this life—when there are so many others who have nothing?

Only God knows the answer to that. And none of it matters in light of eternal rewards. If we live faithful to what God has given us, He will reward us for that faithfulness. It's conceivable that a child in Nepal who simply helped his brother read the Word will receive the same reward as Paul the Apostle. The lady in Minnesota who taught a Sunday School class diligently and loved her children enthusiastically may well find herself standing with Peter.

I used to despair of ever being first in anything. But as I've studied Scripture, I've discovered this is another way in which God has made rewards universally possible. In heaven, there is no competition. God says, "Each will be rewarded according to his own labor" (I Corinthians 3:8).

That means we compete only against ourselves. Will we use our gifts, abilities, and opportunities wisely—or will we waste them?

9. Simply because God is gracious and generous.

Beyond all these reasons for rewards in heaven, there is one other that outshines them all. Even if none of us did anything worthy of note, a single fact gives us marvelous hope. God is generous and gracious. He enjoys giving simply for the sake of giving.

Consider one Scripture. "God, being rich in mercy, because of His great love with which He loved us...made us alive together with Christ...and raised us up with Him...in order that in the ages to come He might show the surpassing riches of His grace in kindness toward us in Christ Jesus" (Ephesians 2:4-7, NASB).

Look at that word, "surpassing." The word in Greek is the union of two words, *hyper* and *ballo*. We've seen the word, *hyper*, in many expressions. It means to go far beyond the usual, the necessary.

But *ballo* is even more interesting. It suggests "throwing, putting, placing." The farmer "scatters seed"; the tree "drops" fruit (Mark 4:26; Revelation 6:13).

It's as though heaven features these huge mountains of wealth—spiritual, divine, eternal wealth, not just gold and silver—and the Lord Himself is standing up there showering giant handsful of it down upon us.

Several years ago, my father bought a new car for his work. I loved it and often told him so. Three years later, he passed that car on to my mom. She used it for several more years. Shortly before Christmas, 1987, Mom wanted a new car, so Dad asked me if I wanted to buy the old one. I said yes and we clinched a deal for several thousand dollars, which was still a great buy. He made up a "promissory note" which said I would pay the amount during the next few years. I drove off into the sunset marveling at my good fortune.

We agreed that I'd start making payments on the car after Christmas. On Christmas day my family drove up to visit my parents. On the Christmas tree nestled an envelope addressed to my wife and me. I had no idea what to expect, but when I opened it I found our promissory note. Dad had written over it: "Paid in full. Merry Christmas. Love, Mom and Dad."

I was astounded and overjoyed. Yet, I wasn't surprised. My father, all through my life, has been overwhelmingly generous in every context.

That event became an illustration to me of the heart of God. That's His mentality. He gives rewards for all the reasons above. But one stands out beyond them all. He gives rewards simply because He loves us and He loves being generous and gracious to His children. He wants to pour it on—for all eternity! We could never deserve all the rewards He offers, even under a system of perfect justice.

But God is not only just, He's also merciful, loving, gracious, giving, holy. That impels Him to inundate us with His blessings. No Christian need ever fear that our heavenly Father might somehow withhold anything that is best for us. Nothing in this world is truly fair. But in heaven, God reverses throttle. Instead of an unfair earth, we receive a fathomless heaven where "fair" is spelled THE SURPASSING RICHES OF HIS GRACE. That day can't come too soon for any of us.

-5-
The Possibility of Loss

So many of us follow a rainbow, or a cloud, or a dream. We console ourselves with the hope of the good life. Hollywood paints it in cinemascope and pipes it into our living rooms. But the "good life," no matter what Merv Griffin or Johnny Carson says, is a fiction. The only "good life" is eternal life, and that's reserved for Christ's new heaven and earth, not this world.

POSSIBILITY OF TOTAL LOSS
Once our lives are subjected to the divine incineration at the *bema* seat of Christ, something—or nothing—will remain. We'll discover which words and works to which we dedicated our lives were of value or a stubble that burns down to char. How we invest our lives now counts for eternity.

Yet, the Bible speaks of the staggering and terrifying possibility of loss. God gives us two kinds of warnings. One suggests a total loss of everything, even heaven itself. A second states that we can invest our lives in the wrong things.

PAUL
Paul spoke of running in vain (Galatians 2:2), being disqualified from the Christian race (I Corinthians 9:27), and having our works burn up (I Corinthians 3:10-15). He focused on one thing: winning his race, fighting the good fight, finishing his

course, keeping the faith. Yet, even he feared the possibility of facing a judgment that left him with a fistful of charcoal.

While watching the 1988 Olympics, I remember watching a competitor in the Decathlon "false start" three times in a sprint. He was disqualified from the event. Though he had done well in the other categories, his attempt at a medal in the Decathlon was over. He complained bitterly afterward that he had trained four years for this event. He knew he could not go through another four years of training in hope of winning a future Olympics. His lips twisted with anger and grief. "Four years of my life! And now this!" Though his eyes flamed at first with anger, they burned down to a chill hopelessness and defeat. Disqualification for him spelled the end. There would never be another chance.

While I don't believe any single sin or even period of sin necessarily disqualifies a person, Paul's statement sobers us all. The unthinkable remains possible, and what looks impossible could become reality if we ever lose our commitment to running our race with determination and lifelong endurance. Although our salvation is eternally secure with Christ, we can still lose big.

JOHN

The Apostle John spoke of similar problems. In I John 2:28 he exhorted Christians to continue in Christ so that we can be "confident and unashamed" when Christ comes back. What might cause this shame? John's phrase means to "remain in, to continue with" someone. The person who doesn't continue in Christ has decided to stop walking with Him the way he once did.

Have you ever been caught in some wrongdoing by someone whom you respected, even feared? If that person had any kind of power over you—like a parent, employer, or someone else in authority—chances are that you felt intense shame in their presence.

Jesus spoke of this situation in a story about an unfaithful slave left in charge of the master's possessions. The faithful slave ran the master's household diligently while he was gone. But the unfaithful slave beat his fellow slaves, and ate and drank with drunkards. He squandered the master's money. Jesus warned that the slave's master would come on a day when he didn't expect him and would cut him into pieces and put him in hell.

While that story in Matthew 24:45-51 speaks of an unbeliever, John seems to have the same thought about believers in I John 2:28. No one wants to be ashamed when Christ comes. It won't cost us our salvation, but it will cost us regret and great loss. The only way to avoid it is to continue in Christ.

JESUS

Jesus was most emphatic about the possibility not only of loss of rewards, but loss of heaven itself. While the Scriptures teach that no believer can lose his salvation, they do exhort us to make certain we are in God's eternal family. Paul told the Corinthians to examine themselves "to see whether you are in the faith" (II Corinthians 13:5). Peter reminded us to "make your calling and election sure" in II Peter 1:10.

On the one hand, God desires that we bask in the great security of our salvation in Christ. We possess an assured, eternal salvation that can never be torn away (John 10:27-28; Romans 8:38-39).

But in another sense, we're never to take it for granted. We cannot suppose that "we're in" and, therefore, we can live any way we want. The person who claims to be a Christian and yet shows no interest in obedience or keeping God's commands is a "liar" according to I John 2:4-6.

Jesus also warns us that disobedience and sin are reasons for great fear. He speaks of the unfaithful slave being "cut in pieces" (Matthew 24:45-51) and of the slave who hid his gifts in the ground losing everything he had (Matthew 25:28-29). He declares to some He doesn't know them even though they supposedly prophesied, performed miracles, and cast out demons in His name (Matthew 25:12, 7:21-23). Is it possible to come to the end of your race and suddenly realize that all along you've been on the wrong side, in the wrong event?

Many do and biographers have looked back on their lives with disturbed pity and wonder. While they receive fame and fight for the things they want—in the end, they lose. They sell their souls for glitter and gain only garish confetti.

WRONG INVESTMENTS

But beyond being in the wrong race, it's possible for a Christian to invest his life in the wrong things. Yes, he's born again. He's headed for heaven. But what he's pouring his energies and his heart into are, in God's eyes, worthless.

What are those things Scripture says are worthless?

•**Building treasure on earth** (Matthew 6:19-24).

While there is much wisdom in saving and investing money to prepare for retirement or your child's inheritance, Jesus warned that hoarding things specifically to enlarge your own pleasures and possessions is foolish. Sound saving is one thing; trying to create your own world of ease and pleasure is another.

•**Right works done for the wrong reasons** (Matthew 6:1-18).

In the Sermon on the Mount, Jesus condemns performing works supposedly for Him just for show, especially giving to charity, praying, and fasting. The Pharisees loved to parade their spirituality before the gaping world. When they dropped a penny in a beggar's dish, they made such a commotion you'd think the emperor had come to town. When they prayed, they stood with heads bowed and eyes closed on the street corners. People who went by thought they were so holy! And when they fasted, they donned their fasting duds and special sackcloth, and they ladled dust on their heads, then moaned and groaned 'til someone remarked about how spiritual they were. Jesus concluded, "They have their reward in full." What was their reward? That people told them they were spiritual. That's what they wanted, attention from people, and that's what they got.

That was all they got, too. Doing good works for show completely negates the work in God's eyes.

•**Works done outwardly but not inwardly** (Matthew 5:21-48).

In Matthew 5:21-48, Jesus clarified the meaning of a number of God's commandments. People thought if you didn't murder anyone you had kept the eighth commandment. But Jesus told them if they were even angry with someone, they'd broken God's Word. Pharisees believed that so long as they didn't actually commit adultery, they'd fulfilled the seventh commandment. But Jesus assured them that looking at a woman in lust was adultery, too.

In other words, our heart attitude matters. It's fairly easy to keep many of God's commandments outwardly. But the spirit must also submit, or it's a worthless work.

•**Works done purely for self** (Matthew 6:33; Colossians 3:23; Philippians 2:19-21).

It's possible to do good for others, but to be doing it for selfish reasons. If you fly to Africa to nurse people with AIDS because you're trying to pacify some inner guilt, there's little good in it from heaven's perspective. If you tithe because you feel you have to, not because you love the Lord, there's no value in it beyond this world.

•**Choosing what impresses over what edifies** (Luke 10:38-42).

The story about Mary and Martha in Luke 10 intrigues us because it gives us an example of one person working very hard to please Christ and at the same time someone else taking it easy at the Lord's feet. Yet, Mary—at the Lord's feet listening to His teaching—is commended, while Martha—trying so hard to meet the Lord's physical needs—is rebuked. But she's not rebuked for doing what she was doing; rather, for resenting her sister's choice of something better. There's nothing wrong with service. But Jesus' point seems to be that there's a time to serve, and there's a time to sit quietly, to listen, and to worship. Perhaps Martha wanted to impress the Lord with her bluster and bustle. Whichever, putting your nose to the servant-stone isn't necessarily the best choice in all circumstances.

•**Lovelessness** (I Corinthians 13:1-3).

Doing great deeds but having no real love for those you're supposedly serving is worthless in God's eyes. It profits no one.

•**Idle words** (Matthew 12:36-37).

Speaking useless, foolish, or idle words has no value in heaven, and it will incur the Lord's personal condemnation.

•**Sin** (Galatians 5:19-21; I Corinthians 6:9-10).

Naturally, all sin is lost time, lost effort, lost reward. Nothing can make up for it. We can only blot it out by confession and repentance (I John 1:9). Unconfessed, it hinders our fellowship and service for Christ.

BUILDING ON THE FOUNDATION

Still, the arena in which loss looms most possible and probable is through having our life's work burn up. We can build our lives and ministries on the foundation of Jesus Christ. We build on his foundation by taking the truth about Jesus and telling others, teaching them, and discipling them on the basis of it. We are building on the foundation when we teach biblical truth in a Junior High Sunday School class. We build on it as we model the truth before our children and they take that example and apply it in their own lives. We build on it as we feast on the truth ourselves and let it color our conduct in life. Wherever the truth of Jesus touches our lives and through us the lives of others, we're building on His foundation.

But each person's work will ultimately pass through a divine fire. The worthless things will burn up. The eternal things will remain.

The question is: What is wood, hay, and straw? And what

does gold, silver, and precious stones mean?

Dwight L. Moody, the famous 19th century evangelist, walked one day along a Chicago street with his song leader, Ira Sankey. The night before, he had preached a powerful sermon that brought many to the Lord. But as they ambled along, they noticed a man stumbling toward them, obviously drunk. When the man spotted Mr. Moody, he recognized him and cried, "Rev. Moody, I'm one of your converts!"

Moody answered, "Yes, I can see you're one of MY converts, but you're none of the Lord's."

Moody undoubtedly had not preached anything false that previous night. But somehow "his" convert got the wrong message. He was the equivalent of wood, hay, and straw.

FALSE TEACHINGS

Today, the world teems with teachers, radio ministers, lay people, and others who teach on a variety of issues. Some stick very closely to the Bible. But others add many of their own ideas, philosophies, principles, and practices. They exhort us to follow them, but do they lead us to Christ?

Watch out for people who teach any of the following:

•**Philosophy** (Colossians 2:8). In the context, these are people who teach that certain foods shouldn't be eaten or special days should be observed, and that we should worship angels. These people often claim to have had visions. Paul says it's "empty deception." Perhaps he foresaw precisely what we have today in the New Age philosophies.

This also refers to humanistic theories and ideas that preachers and teachers promote. Bookstores overflow with volumes citing "ten steps to success" and "five ways to have a happy marriage" and "a hundred ideas for overcoming (name your problem)." Because the author or speaker can crank out a few inspirational stories with it, he thinks he must have something.

But if what he's come up with is "self-made" and not based on solid research and biblical truth, what does he have?

In a word, nothing. It's worthless. Why give your life to it? Why not invest in the real riches?

•**Speculations** (II Timothy 2:23; I Timothy 1:4; John 3:25; I Timothy 6:6). Speculation leads to questions, debates, and arguments. Endless genealogies, mythology, quarreling over religious traditions, and supposed prophesies about the future are all useless. While we should defend the truth, spending years of our lives coming up with counter-arguments and fighting off the critics often accomplishes little.

•**Myths** (I Timothy 1:4; II Peter 1:6). Have you ever heard the true definition of an "anecdote"? It's a story about a famous person which makes funny or inspirational reading, and often brings tears, but really never happened! How we like to embellish, add to, exaggerate, build on, and pump up the things we say!

In 1912, a man named Charles Dawson found a fossilized cranium and jaw at Barkham Manor in Piltdown Common near Lewes, England. On the basis of this find, scientists proposed whole new theories about evolution. Scholars argued for decades over the meaning of this "great" and "important" find. But 40 years later, scientists discovered this was nothing but an incredible fraud foisted on the public and the scientific community.

Strange as that story is, many Christians build their lives on similar myths. What kinds? For instance, as a young Christian I learned about something called "being slain in the Spirit." People told me this was the quintessence of spiritual experience. I witnessed it in a church service. The pastor touched a man on the head, and, suddenly, he crumpled to the ground. At first unconscious, he then babbled away in "tongues." In some circles this practice takes the form of high doctrine. But the Bible never speaks of such an experience as a possibility let alone a doctrine. It's a "myth."

Other people believe in "theistic evolution" and "the gospel of health, wealth, and success." In some churches, ministers wear collars. Some try to date the coming of Christ or prove the identity of the Antichrist or attach the numbers 666 to someone living now. All these come under the heading of speculations and myths. They're useless, foolish pursuits for the committed Christian.

But myths can also apply to our present day fascination with the media. While some "escapes" are good and helpful at times, spending your life watching soap operas and sitcoms, reading reams of romantic novels, mysteries, westerns, and so on, or living for the next video is giving your life to myths. I remember one young man, who, when the movie *E.T.* came out, saw it 26 times. And that was just the first year!

We've given ourselves over to mythic figures—James Bond, Batman, E.T., Teenage Mutant Turtles, and Luke Skywalker—rather than to the real heroes in our everyday lives who demonstrate faith, courage, godliness, and love.

•**Genealogies** (I Timothy 1:4; Titus 3:9). Many Jews enjoyed tracing their precise ancestry. It gave them a certain status.

There are a series of early books, written shortly after the New Testament, called the "pseudepigraphica," the false writings. One is called "The Life of Adam and Eve" and purports to tell of events in Adam and Eve's life after their expulsion from the Garden of Eden. In addition, the "Apocrypha," a number of books written between the end of the Old Testament and the beginning of the New, contains stories of people's lives which are neither accurate nor inspired. Building our lives on these teachings is foolish. Yet, it's on these books that doctrines like "purgatory" and "salvation by good works" are based.

•**Taking away from or adding to God's Word** (Matthew 5:17f; Revelation 22:18-19). Scripture warns us earnestly and fiercely that taking away from God's Word as well as adding to it are extremely dangerous. Yet, this is precisely what Mormons, Christian Scientists, the Children of God, the Unification

71

Church, the Jehovah's Witnesses, and numerous other cults have done.

But not only cults practice this. There are authors, preachers, and evangelists who claim that certain parts of the Bible are not for today. Granted, certain rules and laws in the Old Testament were eliminated by the New. But picking and choosing what commands you will follow and others that you won't is foolhardy at best and blasphemous at worst.

I remember talking to a leader in a large church about preaching. He angrily told me that in my preaching I talked too much about sin and the need for repentance. I brought up what Paul said in II Timothy 4:2, that preachers are to "correct, rebuke, and encourage." He calmly told me he didn't think that was the way we were to preach today. It was outdated.

I've known people in ministries who say that the bodily resurrection is a fallacy and not the meaning of Scripture. Some say that Paul's teaching on women in the church is defunct. Others contend that the qualifications for elders in I Timothy 3 and Titus 1 are too strict and should be thrown out. Some believe that "God doesn't expect anyone to believe the myth of creation anymore," that the book of Revelation is a hopeless mess no one can decipher, that no honest pastor "would touch the subject of predestination with a ten-foot pole," that the life of Jesus in the Gospels is mostly made up, and that the Bible doesn't really teach anything important on divorce and remarriage.

The word for such people is found in Revelation 22:18-19.

•**Incorrect interpretations** (II Timothy 2:16-19; Galatians 3:1-5; III John 3-4).

Teaching God's Word is a sacred duty and honor. But to deal with it lightly or inaccurately is a sin that can bring a severe penalty. Of course, no one is perfect and we all make honest mistakes. Few leaders or teachers in the church today have not changed their views from one side to another on certain issues during their lives.

But even though we make honest mistakes, or even foolish ones, the fact remains that we are to be as accurate as we can in what we teach. The position of a teacher of the Bible is a high responsibility, not to be embarked upon with anything less than acute sobriety. Using the Bible for false teaching dishonors Christ. Advising people that all they need do is believe for salvation, and that they needn't worry about things like repentance, obedience, submission, and discipleship is fraught with error—for the speaker and the listener.

WHAT'S POSSIBLE

These examples and problems might lead us to think, "What's the use? Why try? It's all a lost cause!"

Shortly before Mark Twain died, he wrote, "A myriad of men are born; they labor and sweat and struggle....They squabble and scold and fight; they scramble for little mean advantages over each other; age creeps upon them; infirmities follow....Those they love are taken from them, and the joy of life is turned to aching grief. It [the release] comes at last—the only unpoisoned gift earth ever had for them—and they vanish from a world where they were of no consequence...a world which will lament them a day and forget them forever."[1]

Is that our destiny?

Never. Rather, there is reason to rejoice. While there is the possibility of loss, there is also the greater assurance of triumph. Consider the words of some of those who came to the end of life and looked forward to a joyous reception into the heavenlies.

During the crucifixion, as death drew its dark wings over His soul, Jesus said two things. First, "Father, into your hands I commit my spirit" (Luke 23:46). And, finally, "It is finished."

Both are sober words of faith and hope. The first, a word of assurance for the future that He was going into the arms of His Father. The second, a look back on the life already lived. What kind of life? One that had been mapped out and planned in detail by His Father. One that, when He came to the end, He could confidently say, "I have done all that He called me to do" (John 19:30).

Jesus knew His Father and the truth of heaven.

When Peter faced his own end, he wrote in his second epistle, "For if you do these things, you will never fall, and you will receive a rich welcome into the eternal kingdom of our Lord and Savior Jesus Christ" (II Peter 1:10-11). There was a wonderful future ahead for him.

But perhaps the greatest eulogy of confidence in a blessed future came from Paul's pen. He said in II Timothy 4:7-8: "I have fought the good fight, I have finished the race, I have kept the faith. Now there is in store for me the crown of righteousness, which the Lord, the righteous Judge, will award to me on that day—and not only to me, but also to all who have longed for His appearing."

Was this conceit or self-delusion? Was Paul patting himself on the back, and in a moment of pride, betraying a falsely confident spirit?

There are those who suggest that we should never think we've done anything good or lasting. They suppose that Paul's words lack true humility. Or they think that Paul should have tempered his words. "I've tried to fight the good fight. If I've failed, that's my failure. I've tried to run my course. But naturally I've made mistakes. I've tried to keep the faith. I sincerely hope I haven't failed. Now I hope there is a crown of righteousness in store for me. Perhaps Jesus will give it to me, but I certainly have no reason to expect that He will."

Would that have been a humbler, more self-effacing statement?

Perhaps...in human eyes. But that is not what Paul said. "I have fought....I have finished....I have kept....There is in store for me...." Those were unflinching, unwavering, undoubting words of confidence. How could Paul make such a statement—and under the inspiration of the Spirit of God?

There was only one way: because they were true. God let him

74

write his own divine epitaph.

If it's not possible to live a God-honoring life, if it's not probable that any of us alive today can reach the end and say, "I have lived for Jesus"; if it's inconceivable that any person in history besides Jesus Himself could claim to have "kept the faith," then why try? If we can't gain the prize, if we can't win the race, if we can't live lives worthy of reward, then why live them?

This isn't about perfection. Paul knew well his imperfections.

I'm not talking about such high commitment that every day people talk about how "different" you are from the rest of the human race. Paul, Peter, and John all had their bad years, too.

This isn't a level of piety that spends every waking minute in spiritual activity. Paul was a tentmaker. Jesus was a carpenter. Peter and John were fishermen.

But when they came to the end and looked back on the course of their lives, they could confidently declare, "I have fought the good fight." Paul spoke of his fear of disqualification in I Corinthians 9:24-27. He told the Galatians that he was afraid he'd wasted his efforts on them (Galatians 4:11). And at one point he went to Jerusalem with Barnabas to submit his teachings to the scrutiny of Peter and the elders; he was terrified he might be preaching heresy (Galatians 2:1-4).

Yet, at the end, when he could do nothing more in God's fields of harvest, he could honestly—and in the power of the Spirit—say, "I have fought the good fight."

How? I don't understand. I spend many of my waking minutes believing that I'm a washout, a failure, and a source of complete displeasure to God. Yet, perhaps what Paul was seeing was the context of Ephesians 2:10: "We are God's workmanship...." God worked in Paul to accomplish great things. Even though, at some moments in his life, Paul despaired that they counted for anything, yet, at the end he knew he'd fought hard, long, and in a way that pleased God. It wasn't personal pride; it was God's grace. He knew he'd achieved nothing but what God achieved in him. And his words are an anthem of praise to God, not himself.

In the same way, God has not destined us for "loss." Even now His Holy Spirit labors inside us to enable us to "fight the good fight." None of us has to live with the expectation of loss. Yes, we should soberly face the possibility. But we shouldn't live in a despair, as though it has already happened. More than once Jesus said "the last shall be first." And it may well be that many of the small, quiet deeds done in small, quiet places will be revealed as scintillating diamonds in His glorious crown.

FOOTNOTES
[1] "A Striking Contrast" by Herb VanderLugt, *Our Daily Bread* (Grand Rapids, MI: Radio Bible Class), April 24, 1980. Used by permission.

-6-
The Rewards Motive

On occasion people react with anger and even vehemence at the idea of serving God for rewards. They say, "We should serve God out of love for Him, not because He will reward us." Some assert, "Doing something that's good and right because you believe God will bless you in some way is crass. That's the health, wealth, and prosperity gospel." And others answer, "It sounds like a tit for tat kind of thing. 'I do this; God does that.' I don't like it."

If we were talking about some kind of "you scratch my back, I'll scratch yours" situation where our "reward" is immediate and guaranteed based on our actions, perhaps those claims would hold. However, the Bible never guarantees that God will reward us for our works in this lifetime. In fact, Paul told us that "everyone who wants to live a godly life in Christ Jesus will be persecuted" (II Timothy 3:12). Doing good, speaking truth, and living righteously may not receive a blessing in this world; it could invoke a curse. The first Christians went to the lions. The last Christians will suffer at the hands of the Antichrist. Where does that put us in-between?

KINDS OF MOTIVATION

God holds a promise out to each of us. "If you forsake a job on Wall Street in order to take Jesus to the homeless, I will reward you a hundred times whatever you might have gained in this world" (*cf.* Matthew 19:29). "If you fight a good fight and endure as My disciple, I will give you a crown" (*cf.* II Timothy 4:6-8). "If you stay in the faith and don't give up, I will let you reign with Me" (*cf.* II Timothy 2:11-13).

What is God trying to do? In a word, motivate us. How does anyone, including God, move Christians to action? How does He get us to serve Him sacrificially?

Look at some of the motivational techniques Jesus used while on earth. Jesus walked up to Peter and Andrew, said something to them, and they left their nets to follow Him. In effect, they dumped their jobs, their security, and even their foreseeable future in order to travel through the hills with Jesus and learn from Him. Why? Jesus said to them, "Follow Me, and I will make you fishers of men" (Mark 1:17). He gave a promise in response to His call. "Do this for Me, and I will do that for you."

Was this an appeal to selfish, crass, fleshly humanity? No, on the contrary, Jesus' promise offered little more than an assurance of trouble, trial, and testing. Yet, Peter and Andrew responded positively to His words. They wanted what He offered...no matter what the cost.

FEAR

There are a number of levels of motivation in our world which both leaders, speakers, and even the Bible uses to move us to action. Probably the lowest level of motivation is simple fear. "If you don't do this, I'll fire you!" Fear of the consequences of not doing what we're asked can be a potent force towards change. It's not a very good means of motivation. And sometimes it leads to rebellion and a fight.

But even the Bible shows this kind of tactic. Remember when God met with Moses on Mount Sinai? He warned the people not to come near the mountain or even to touch it, or they would die (Exodus 19:12). Jesus told His disciples, "Unless you repent, you too will all perish" (Luke 13:3). The process of church discipline carries a high note of fear in its warnings (Matthew 18:15-17). John warned Diotrephes that he would come and confront him in the presence of the church if he didn't cease his divisive teaching and malicious gossip (III John 9-10). Even Paul realized there was a penalty if he did not obey God's calling for his life to preach the gospel (I Corinthians 9:16-17).

Fear can be a good motivator and, at times, a worthy one. God uses it in many cases to keep us from sin. When we choose to obey Him because we fear the consequences of disobedience, we're making an intelligent choice.

But it's not the only reason why we do what we do.

IMMEDIATE REWARD

A second level of motivation is founded in the concept of immediate reward.

Again, the Scriptures express this brand of get up and go. Through Moses, God assured the people that if they obeyed Him, all sorts of earthly rewards would follow, including exaltation over other nations, healthy offspring, productive fields, defeated enemies, and constant prosperity (Deuteronomy 28:1-14). Confession of sin brings immediate and permanent forgiveness (Psalm 103:12; I John 1:9). Jesus called the disciples with the promise that He would make them fishers of men (Mark 1:17).

All of us operate on this level. We show up at our place of work because we know that at specific times of the month we'll receive a paycheck for our efforts. A lady diets because she's convinced she'll end up with a healthy, beautiful body. A salesman hurries along his route mastering the best techniques in marketing because his employer promises to give him ten, twenty, or thirty percent of the profits.

Even our instincts function on the basis of immediate reward. Hungry? Go to the 'fridge and get your chocolate urge filled. Tired and weary? Lie down in your soft bed and soon sweet dreams will whisk away all the fatigue.

It's a powerful source of *oomph* and Madison Avenue has used it to heist billions from our pockets. But again, it's a lower form of motivation that, while effective, does not bring out the best in us. It's more along the lines of "what do I get out of it—today?"

GRATITUDE

A third level of motivation comes under the heading of gratitude. We obey Jesus or someone else as a thank you for all they've done for us. Christ forgave us and gave us eternal life. We're so overwhelmed with joy and thanks that we want to serve Him with our lives.

What is worship except praise and gratitude for who He is? It all comes down to His worth in our eyes. He has done so much for us that somehow we must return the favor. Gratitude, worship, praise, adoration, and thanksgiving make favorable and worthy responses.

Yet, this isn't something we do only in a spiritual sense. Which of us has not given a gift in gratitude to someone for a kindness they did on our behalf? What is the motivation behind a thank you note, or a word of praise to a speaker, or a hug for Grandma on Christmas Day? Gratitude motivates us to some of our highest acts of goodness.

LOVE

Beyond all this, though, we find the motivation of love. We obey Christ simply because we love Him. Jesus said, "If you love me, you will obey what I command" (John 14:15). In the same passage, He said, "If anyone loves me, he will obey my teaching. My Father will love him, and we will come to him and make our home with him" (14:23).

Love is a powerful motivator, and it may be the highest.

ETERNAL REWARDS AS A MOTIVATION

What, then, should we say about the reality of eternal

rewards as a divine and biblical motivation? These are not immediate rewards because we receive no guarantee of payback for our goodness in this time and place. Rather, they are the promise of great rewards *after* we've finished this life. They're way out there in the future somewhere. We can't see them. We can't feel or, in some ways, even comprehend them. But we have it on God's word that they're there; they are worth the effort, and they will never cease to make us marvel at God's grace.

Where do these figure in our hierarchy of motivation?

Suppose a Christian begins obeying and living for the Lord because he believes God will ultimately reward him in the new heavens and the new earth? Suppose he begins making decisions—choosing the godly and holy activity over the sinful or worthless ones—because he believes that God will ultimately commend him in heaven? Where does that figure into the picture? Is it crass? Is it impudent? Is such a motivation and expectation a low rung form of incentive? Or is it the highest form of giving glory to the Lord now, while we're on earth?

To answer this question, I believe we must consider one important scriptural truth about rewards at the outset: **God Himself emphasizes rewards.**

Clearly, the Lord considers the offer of heavenly rewards an important promise or He wouldn't make so many of them. Why has He given it such prominence? Why did He tell the disciples that those who left father, mother, or their homes to serve Him would receive a hundred times as much in His kingdom (Matthew 19:29)? If He thought it might be vain or selfish, why would He appeal to such truth?

I believe there have been times in my life when I've obeyed the Lord out of pure fear. For instance, one sin I fear greatly is adultery. I'm convinced that if I ever did it, God would deal with me as He did with David: after I repented, there would be forgiveness but also some terrible consequences. My motivation in that area is, very frankly, sheer, unadulterated, mind-numbing terror. I pray that motivation stays lodged in me forever.

There are also times when I have obeyed the Lord because I know it's the right and good thing to do. The Scriptures make it clear that being kind and loving is "good" in itself. I don't need someone dumping a hundred dollars at my feet to get me to pat my daughter on the head and tell her I love her. The Lord doesn't have to come alongside and promise me a diamond in my crown if I'll just visit Grandmom over at the nursing home. It's a good and right thing to do. And that's enough.

In addition, I've witnessed, taught Bible studies, and served in ministries simply out of gratitude for all He's done for me. It's a way to say thank you.

Finally, there are times when I have chosen to do good from what I believe was a pure heart of love. Many times I have prayed for long periods because I love the Lord and wanted— craved—that fellowship with Him. Those times are enriching, jubilant, fun. I weep, I laugh, and the time goes quickly. My heart overflows. I have spent hours studying the Bible, reading godly books, and preaching sermons because my love for Him seems like a geyser spewing pure water through my soul.

But then there are times like now when I struggle with writing books and articles for Christians when I know I could be on my way to working a six figure job, selling some worthy product. Non-Christians have told me I'm persuasive and could sell anything I wanted and probably make a lot of money if I worked at it. At other times, people have advised me to forget writing religious books. "You'll never make much money doing that. If you want a real bestseller, quit talking about all this Jesus stuff. Write a thriller or a solid mystery. You could make a mint." So why do I stumble around in Christian publishing with a much smaller income?

Quite frankly, that's where the idea of rewards comes in. If I didn't believe that doing what I do pleases God and would result in some benefit—i.e., an eternal reward—I'd have to ask,

"Why do it?"

Yes, we should serve the Lord simply because He is worthy. We should love Him because He commands it. We should obey Him because obedience is right and good, and His commandments are holy and true. Plain gratitude ought to be enough to motivate us to follow Him for all eternity. But sooner or later, all of us ask, "What's in it for me?"

Is that an unspiritual question? Is that selfish, ignoble, unholy, sinful? Is it the height of arrogance to expect that God might give us something good if we go His way, if we deny ourselves in this world, and serve Him all out?

It can't be, because that's the way He's designed it. He has put rewards on the heavenly agenda. He reminds us of them constantly in His Word. He wants us to know, "Hey, there is something in it for you! I intend to pay you back—handsomely! When it will really count."

It's not a tit for tat kind of idea, either. It's not, "If I visit this widow, God's going to give me a crown." It's not, "If I give this dollar, God will give me a hundred." We needn't go around performing good deeds only because we're convinced God will "heap it on" when we get to heaven. Actually, the idea of rewards is an act of grace. We can't ever really deserve anything from Him. How can we accomplish anything that's good that He, by His Spirit, didn't work in us?

Some Christians may deceive themselves into thinking that they serve God from such a pure heart that it never occurs to them that they will get anything out of it. Well, we can all banish such thoughts. The very reason we came to Jesus was because we wanted forgiveness, cleansing, salvation, and eternal life. Jesus said, "Come to Me, and I will give you rest." Jesus didn't say, "Believe in Me because I am worthy and that should be enough." No. He said, "He who believes in Me, from His innermost being shall flow rivers of living water." Take almost any command of God and there is some benefit for the one who obeys it.

God is that way. Although He doesn't need the world, creation, or any of us, He receives a benefit from our love, our worship, and our faith. Otherwise, why would He ask for it? If it's totally meaningless to Him, then what's the point?

God encourages us to realize there's plenty in it for all of us. He doesn't do that to encourage selfishness; rather, He does it to encourage us to become completely *un* selfish. He tells us that He will reward us for loving our neighbors, doing good deeds to our enemies, and giving money to support people in the ministry. Ultimately, what He's doing is trying to rid us of *self-*ishness. He's saying. "Stop trying to get everything for yourself. Instead, look to Me, follow Me, obey Me, serve Me, and I will reward you beyond anything you might be able to drum up on your own in this world!" He's trying to turn our minds away from this world, away from taking all we can from everyone else, and to put us in an attitude that looks completely to Him for every good gift.

That's the essence of faith and love for God—relying on Him completely for everything.

If you are a parent, think about the kinds of motivation you use with your children. How many times do you offer some benefit you know your child wants in exchange for obedience in some area? I told my six-year-old daughter the other day that if she gave me a free hour for writing, I'd take her for a walk and stop at the playground on the way. She not only gave me my hour, but excitement and happiness glowed on her face as we walked together.

When it comes to rewards, Jesus doesn't want us to think how we can get more than others or to be exalted over others. He rebuked His disciples primarily for their arrogance when they argued about who was the greatest (Matthew 18:1-4). When James and John sent their mother to ask for the left and right hand seats next to His throne, Jesus told them they neither knew what they were asking nor how evil their hearts were (Mark 10:35-45).

But God wants us to understand that following Him isn't a matter of obligation or duty. He doesn't want our loyalty at the point of a threat. What He desires is that we be friends, lovers, and worshipers who honor Him from a heart of love, joy, and gratitude. What better way to promote such feelings than through giving good things to those you love? After all, isn't our inclination to give, love, serve, help, and meet needs an expression of His image? It's for that reason that I don't think God offers rewards to us just to motivate us; I believe He does it because He loves giving good things to His children.

Being motivated by rewards demonstrates total faith and trust in God, which is necessary to please Him (Hebrews 11:6). Think of it! A widow gives every cent she has because she believes that honors God. A young married man decides to work hard at controlling his temper and loving a nagging, belligerent wife because he wants to please God.

What would the world say about such people? "Pie in the sky!" "Foolishness." "Get what you can now, and forget the cloud with the silver lining!" The world often regards people who sacrifice and give their lives for God's values as the ultimate fools because they have little proof that what they're doing will succeed.

If someone pays a hundred dollars to win the Lotto Jackpot, we might call him a gambler, or we might say he's wasting his money. But if we give that hundred dollars to print tracts for spreading the gospel, though some would commend us, many would think we're wasting our hard-earned dollars: better to use it on a stock investment or to save it for our child's college education.

Being motivated by eternal rewards requires tremendous faith on a level far beyond the norm. We are literally staking our lives, our money, our time, and our efforts on God's Word. Wouldn't the Lord be pleased by such faith?

When we're motivated by eternal rewards, we're also showing fear and respect for God. Remember Jacob and

Esau? What did Esau sell his birthright—the right to the first son's inheritance—for? A mess of stew! Was that a demonstration of respect and reverence for his father, Isaac? Was that a reflection of the high esteem he felt for his family heritage? By no means. Rather, it showed how little he respected everyone and everything.

In the same way, suppose a father collects stamps. He enjoys it and has one of the best collections on earth. Now imagine that he says to his three sons, "I'll give equal parts of that collection to each of my sons who go out, do good, and obey the principles I live by." One son says, "Who cares about those old stamps? I'd rather have fun." The second son says, "I know the stamps are valuable, so when I get them I'll sell them off and make a mint." But the third son knows how important those stamps are to his Dad. Though he's not an avid collector himself, he decides, "Since Dad thinks so highly of this collection, I'll try to do as he says. Who knows, maybe I'll discover that I like stamp collecting myself!"

Which son showed real respect for his father?

Similarly, when we obey God on the basis of His promised rewards, even though we may not understand the rewards He offers, we are showing Him true respect. We're demonstrating that we think highly of Him as our God!

Above all, acting on the basis of those promised rewards demonstrates deep and abiding love for the Father. Obviously, God considers rewards important. Clearly, He wants to give us His best. He longs to shower upon us every good thing. When we love what He loves, when we care about what He cares about, we're really showing that we care about Him.

WHERE REWARD MOTIVATION FITS IN

Whether we do what we do out of fear, a sense of duty, gratitude, love, the hope of rewards, or some other reason, the fact is that God accepts them all. He knows that we're all different and He's provided a way to meet each of our needs.

That's enough to help me trek onward. Knowing that one day I will stand before Him gives me fear. Knowing that one day He might say to me, "Well done," gives me hope and exhilaration. But knowing that He longs to fill my eternity with every good gift opens my heart to awe, reverence, joy, and love.

Truly, His greatness is fathomless!

-7-
Rewarded for Loving Christ or Serving Christ?

The back cover of J.I. Packer's classic work on *Knowing God* reads:

What were we made for? To know God.

What aim should we set ourselves in this life? To know God.

What is the eternal life that Jesus gives? Knowledge of God.

What is the best thing in life? Knowledge of God.

What in man gives God most pleasure? Knowledge of Himself.[1]

For many Christians, the essence of their spiritual lives revolves around such activities as church worship, having a "quiet time," memorizing Bible verses, reading the Bible and other books on faith and life, spending time in prayer and adoration of God, and "praying without ceasing." I personally consider all these elements important and indispensable aspects of Christian living which no sensible believer can discard or neglect.

But when we speak of rewards—the fact that we'll all "receive what is due him for the things done while in the body, whether good or bad," as II Corinthians 5:10 says—how do these things figure? Will God actually reward us for the amount of time and effort we put into having a quiet time? If we have memorized a thousand verses and another person has memorized four thousand, will each receive a different reward?

During my own Christian life, I have logged many hours in prayer, Bible study, and memorization, even to the exclusion of other activities. Should I count on a mention of this at the *bema*? "Joe Tibbs memorized 3,206 verses during his Christian walk! What a great guy!"

"Jane Larsen faithfully executed a forty-five minute quiet time every day for 37 years! Hallelujah!"

In other words, will God actually reward us for how well we knew Him while on earth?

PRELIMINARIES

This is a ticklish issue and not a subject entered into lightly. Perhaps several beginning thoughts will help.

First, the Pharisees concentrated on spiritual disciplines such as prayer, Bible study, and fasting. Yet, Jesus called them hypocrites. Why? Because they knew the facts, but they failed to apply them to their lives. They dutifully performed the sacrifices and rituals, but they held their hearts back from God. They obediently kept much of the law, yet hated their enemies, ignored those who hurt, spurned anyone less "spiritual," and exalted themselves above everyone but their own kind.

This is a trap Christians easily fall into. We diligently practice our quiet times, but we forget the poor or hungry. We tithe our ten percent, yet we sacrifice little in love or inconvenience. What is the difference between a businessman who reads his Bible in his office, then slams around his employees—and a Pharisee that Jesus called "a viper"? How can a housewife who prays an hour every morning and then gossips on the phone all afternoon say she's pleasing God?

The fact is that spiritual disciplines without resultant life changes are meaningless. It never pleases God for us to keep our quiet time and abuse our family, friends, or the clerk at the store. If necessary, Jesus would probably say, "Forget the quiet time and treat your wife and others right!" God even refuses to hear the prayers of husbands who dishonor their wives (I Peter 3:7).

Second, spiritual disciplines act as means to an end, not as ends in themselves. David said he meditated on Scripture to gain security and produce fruit (Psalm 1:1-3). God told Joshua to meditate on the law not simply to know it, but in order to apply it to the problems of life (Joshua 1:8). We treasure the word in our hearts not to pile up verses but so that we might not sin against God (Psalm 119:11). Knowing the Word guides and directs us through the difficulties of our days (Psalm 119:105; Proverbs 6:20-23).

Yes, we should observe spiritual disciplines. They strengthen, build, guide, perfect, and establish us more firmly in our faith. They'll lead us through a tangle of temptations with triumph. They ground us in holy living. But we can't view them as works that God will reward us for, like the Pharisees did. Jesus said He would reward us for our almsgiving, prayer, and fasting only when our hearts are right, and only as we do these secretly, out of love for God, not the expectation of reward (Matthew 6:1-14).

Third, even salvation is not an end in itself. Paul told Titus that Jesus "gave himself for us to redeem us from all wickedness and to purify for himself a people that are his very own, eager to do what is good" (Titus 2:14). This is why preachers who offer salvation without mentioning the need for repentance, transformation, and growth are such an abomination to God. No real Christian can walk an aisle, claim eternal life, and sashay away with no thought for a lifetime change, turning from sin, fellowship with God, and obedience.

Compare salvation to a person who decides to get married. He chooses freely. He receives through marriage tremendous gifts. But the relationship changes him. He's no longer just himself, without responsibilities. His life has undergone a complete reversal, a revolution.

Similarly, a man or woman who trusts Christ will change. As

in a marriage, the relationship brings with it both privileges and responsibilities. The interaction forces him to accommodate, compromise, accept, and forgive. His inner life is transfigured. He's no longer who he used to be.

Fourth, knowing God and faith both please God, but without works both are useless. James said, "In the same way, faith by itself, if it is not accompanied by action, is dead" (James 2:17). James devotes the whole second half of James 2 to the issue of faith and works. The Holy Spirit led him—and us—to the conclusion that faith must lead to works and life change or it's not real faith, not the kind Jesus came to give us.

In Hebrews 11, sometimes called the "Faith Hall of Fame," look at what the writer focuses on: "By faith, Abel offered....By faith, Noah...built an ark....By faith, Abraham...obeyed and went....By faith, Isaac blessed...." Faith leads to action. Knowing God leads to worship, adoration, love, compassionate treatment of others, fear of committing sin, holiness of life, and the doing of good.

Have we exchanged a false spirituality—burnt offerings and sacrifices, quiet times and memory verses—in neglect of the greater requirements of God's holy law—compassion, kindness, generosity, and patience (Matthew 23:23-39)?

This doesn't mean we shouldn't have a quiet time or memorize verses or pray. But all of those disciplines are meant to lead to transformed attitudes and actions. If they do not, what good are they?

SOME CONCLUSIONS

What can we conclude from these thoughts?

1. The purpose of our relationship with God through spiritual disciplines is a friendship and a fellowship meant to be enjoyed, not a commodity to be rewarded.

What God desires is that we enjoy His friendship, Father to son and daughter. And, just as a father showers his children with gifts out of love, so God will do for us. But it has nothing to do with rewards.

2. Spiritual disciplines should be practiced with an eye to life application. Memorizing verses should change our lives as we apply them to the problems of life. Knowing and learning of God is a joy that leads us to go out and let His life shine through us in all kinds of goodness, kindness, self-discipline and understanding. Our Bible study is a means for us to know Him better and in so doing transform us and energize us. It isn't something God will add up in terms of hours and years and duly reward.

3. No matter how great the rewards are that God promises to give us, simply knowing Him is the greatest joy and reward of all. Knowing and being known by Him rank far higher than white stones, hidden manna, responsibility for five cities, and a bumper crop of crowns. Even though we should take rewards seriously, building our relationship with Him through spiritual disciplines generates the real gems of Christian life. Paul spurned all his earthly honors in comparison to the "surpassing greatness of knowing Christ Jesus my Lord" (Philippians 3:8). David thirsted after God like the deer panting for water (Psalm 42:1-2).

Truly knowing Him is what it's all about. The gift of Himself outshines all others. They're mere trinkets next to standing in His loving presence and experiencing His friendship.

Spiritual disciplines are a means to two ends:

to know God first.

to serve God second.

If the disciplines do not affect us in this way, we need to reevaluate. Am I doing them for the wrong reasons?

We must examine the actional, or works, element of our walk with Christ. God solemnly charges us to obey, serve, give, and love both for Him and through Him. The works we do in His name matter. He will reward us for what we have done in the body.

But the greatest reward is Himself—and He is free. We cannot earn Him. We cannot win a friendship with Him through doing good. We cannot use our minutes in prayer as a cudgel to force Him to love us.

No, we gain Him only through faith, through taking Him at His word and entering the relationship as one embarks upon a marriage. He longs to be our confidante, our lover, our friend, and our eternal guide. We can't purchase that relationship at any price. We can only receive it as a gift. Undoubtedly, it's the greatest gift of all.

FOOTNOTES
[1]James I. Packer, *Knowing God* (InterVarsity Press, Downer's Grove, IL, 1973).

SECTION THREE:
What Counts In the Here and Now?

-8-

Good Works Are Fine, But I'm Not Perfect

What are good works?

I worked on an article about church life for a large national magazine. My editor and I rewrote it five times. She suggested I needed a powerful illustration of sacrifice. I finally unearthed one in a story about a young worker in a leper colony in India. One night her leaders preached a joyous message saying that when you nursed the body of a leprous person, you touched the body of Christ.

With great enthusiasm, the young nurse went out and found a man lying in a gutter. Maggots covered his rotting flesh. His face was virtually peeled away, leaving nothing but stumps and ugly clots of flesh. Obviously, he was dying. But the girl resisted the urge to run and helped him. She lifted him to a grassy place, bandaged his wounds, and spoke gently and kindly to him. Even his dim eyes lit with joy as he saw her genuine concern and interest. When the young nurse next saw her mission leader, an ecstasy filled her as she held up her hands and exclaimed, "I have been touching the body of Christ."

It was a moving story for me. But when I shared it with my editor she laughed and said, "I went to a religious high school and all during those years I heard about missionaries brushing maggots off dying people and working in the stench of the leper colonies as an act of mercy. I'm sorry, Mark, but we need something a little less unusual and something most of us can identify with."

Her thoughts jarred me. Indeed, what is a "good work"? Is is something on the level of Albert Schweitzer? William Carey? Mother Teresa? Does one have to fly to a plague-ridden locale of the world and scrape off flies and vermin to qualify as a worker of good works? Do you have to sacrifice everything by plunging into the jungles of darkest Africa? In other words, can a businessman working in a machinery company hope to do a truly "good work" in the business context?

Can a housewife with a headache and three kids in the sandbox do something that God would consider "worthy of eternal rewards"?

Can a recently retired grandfather who likes working in the garden serve God?

Can a young construction roofer consider his life worth anything beyond this world?

There is a lot of confusion about good works in our contemporary faith and practice. At one time as a Boy Scout I heard that good deeds were things like "helping little old ladies and children across the street." Try as I did, I rarely had the opportunity to help any little old ladies across the street, though there were a few children here and there. Most of them seemed willing and able to care for themselves.

At other times I have imagined good deeds to be stupendous acts of sacrifice and grace. Have you ever imagined leaping in front of a car to save a child from death? Maybe it was Hollywood's effect on me, but picturing myself as a hero gave me a deep sense of thrill and joy. Ah, the bliss of expending your life in a noble act! Of course, it has never happened. Maybe I need to spend more time on the lookout.

Still another variation is the "final act of goodness" in a lost life. In this scenario, we know the bad guy has a truly decent heart, and though he's done evil all his life, at the end, he suddenly changes character and performs an ultimate act of good that saves everyone. Sidney Carton in *A Tale of Two Cities*, having lived a debauched life, saves his friend, Charles Darnell, from death by exchanging places with him in prison shortly before going to the guillotine. Carton says in the end, "It is a far, far better thing that I do, than I have ever done; it is a far, far better rest that I go to, than I have ever known." The final good deed in an otherwise non-spectacular or even evil life makes it all worth it.

Another type of good deed is like the one at the beginning of this chapter, when someone does something good in an environment or situation that is so disgusting and repulsive any normal person would shrink from it. Somehow the fact that we did it against such a backdrop makes the deed that much more holy and beautiful.

Do any of these "really count" for eternity? What does the Bible say?

We need to be clear about something at the start. Without faith in Christ as our Savior, all our "good deeds" are "filthy rags" in the eyes of God (Isaiah 64:6). Apart from Christ, we can do nothing that has real value in the eyes of God (John 15:5).

Some may find it hard to accept, but no matter how decent, loving, and kind we appear on the surface, no matter how much the world may praise us or award us Nobel Prizes or other accolades, if we do not believe and follow Jesus as our Savior, Lord, King, and Friend, nothing we ever do will count. The whole world may praise people like Martin Luther King, Albert Schweitzer, Bishop Tutu, Mother Teresa, and others. But if those individuals do not have Christ residing in their hearts, if they have not fallen at His feet confessing their sin and receiving His salvation—it doesn't matter what they have done; God rejects it.

I'm not saying these people weren't or aren't born-again

Christians; I don't know that one way or the other. I'm certainly not in the position to make such a judgment; only Christ can know that. But Jesus Himself accused the Pharisees—the greatest good deed doers of the world at that time—of being children of the devil (John 8:42-44). At the Great White Throne Judgment there will be people who will cry out, "Lord, Lord, did we not prophesy in your name, and in your name drive out demons and perform many miracles?" What will be His response to these "do-gooders"? "I never knew you. Away from me, you evildoers" (Matthew 7:22-23).

It's quite possible to be a good, loving, decent, kind, altruistic, and even "religious" person and not know Jesus personally. Apart from a sincere and genuine faith in Christ, it's all a waste of time.

TWO WORDS

Still, we need to understand what the Bible says is a good deed. The New Testament uses two Greek words we translate "good." The first is *kalos*. It means something that is good in itself, something intrinsically good. By contrast, the Greek word *agathos* means "good in character or constitution."[1] It's beneficial to others.

Both words are used in reference to a good deed or "work" in the Bible. So let's look at a number of acts in Scripture which qualify as "good deeds."

•**Helping others in need** (Matthew 25:34-40; James 1:27). Jesus spoke often of our responsibility to give food to the hungry, to give a drink to a thirsty man, hospitality to a stranger, clothes to the naked, company to the sick, and friendship to those in prison. James speaks of visiting "orphans and widows in their distress." Many of these acts are so simple, it seems preposterous that God would single them out for mention. But this is the very heart of the deed that is *good* in God's eyes. They are, by their nature, things each of us can do. They're not stupendous. They don't even involve a monumental sacrifice in

97

time or money. But God views these things as good deeds worthy of commendation.

•**Receiving the followers of Christ** (Matthew 10:41). When we invite other people into our homes to listen to them, give them lodging, and show hospitality, we are doing a good deed. When we open our homes to missionaries, ministers, or others who travel about proclaiming the gospel, we are obeying God. Jesus says in that text we "will receive a righteous man's reward." Furthermore, practicing this with strangers (III John 5-6) and people we don't even know (Hebrews 13:2-3) pleases God.

•**Doing justice, loving kindness, walking with God** (Micah 6:8). This verse covers a lot of ground. Yet, things like justice are so uncommon in our world. Treating people kindly is often so astonishing that whole movies are made and books written about people who lead lives of unselfish goodness and kindness.

Authors have chronicled in recent days the lives and deeds of people like Corrie ten Boom, Eric Liddell, Dr. Viggo Olsen, and Kefa Sempangi as examples of men and women who sacrificed their time, money, and in some cases their lives, to do good in our world. But this is not something reserved for the famous. Fame in this world doesn't insure "fame" in eternity. The Christian woman who works for justice in her community, the volunteer on the Pregnancy Center Hotline, and the man who donates money to a mission organization are practicing the good deeds of justice and kindness as much as any of those we read about.

•**Letting your light shine** (Matthew 5:16). Jesus said we are to "let our light shine before men." How? By letting people see our good works. The principle might be summarized: "Let the world know that you're a Christian by treating others with kindness and love. Make the doing of good to all—in thought, word, and deed—the quality of your life. They'll notice, even if they don't say so. But be sure you re-direct any praise for it to the Father. It's rightfully His."

• **Special gifts to Jesus** (Matthew 26:10). When Mary broke the vial of perfume and poured it on Jesus' head, some complained. But Jesus told them she had done a beautiful thing to Him.

In the same way, when we do anything as a special act of love and devotion to Christ, it ranks as a good deed in God's eyes. Whether it's a season of prayer, a monetary donation to a Christian organization, or a simple word of thanks and love to Him, it all pleases God and He promises to reward us.

I have a friend who, on Christmas day, always sings "Happy Birthday" to Jesus. Another person writes poetry specifically for Him. A third, whenever she gives someone a monetary gift, always says, "I give it to you in the name of Jesus." Some people disdain such piety, but if you have children, you know how much you appreciate the little gifts they bring to you—the drawings, the cards, the dandelions pulled from the yard. Think how much more the Lord must enjoy our attempts to show Him love!

• **Doing the works Jesus did** (John 10:32). Jesus spoke of the "great miracles" He had shown to others: miraculous healings, casting out demons, raising the dead, turning water into wine. We cannot perform these deeds, but there are human counterparts. When we do things for others without an expected return (meaning not being paid for it), but out of love and goodness, we are doing "the works of Jesus."

A woman I know visited a shut-in for many years before the lady died. This determined woman read whole books to her over the course of several visits. She chatted. She was a friend. Her only payment in this world was whatever personal joy and fulfillment she got out of it. But Jesus knows what she did. I think she'll find her reward from Him.

• **Leading others** (I Timothy 3:1). Paul speaks of being an elder as a "good work." Diligence in leading and governing the flock brings with it a high reward, but it is also an awesome responsibility. For that reason, the Bible says leaders will bear a stricter judgment and "give an account" of how they led others (James 3:1, Hebrews 13:17). But Peter also assures those who lead well that they will receive a crown of glory (I Peter 5:2-4). God promises to reward elders in a worthy and memorable way.

•Bringing up children, showing hospitality, washing the saints' feet, assisting those in distress, devoting oneself to every good work (I Timothy 5:10). Paul pointed out that widows who wanted to devote themselves to God's service and "be placed on the list" should overflow with "good works." His list is especially interesting in that it includes acts we might not normally think of as good deeds. But things like bringing up children, serving others, being hospitable, opening your home to people, and helping people in distress qualify.

This is also a great word to mothers and fathers. One of the greatest deeds we can bring to the Lord's feet is raising children in the faith, nurturing them, and building godly character into their lives. The home provides an excellent ground for practicing our faith, doing the wonderful deeds of love and kindness that catch God's eyes, and establishing a bounty of righteousness that will last into eternity.

•Being generous (I Timothy 6:17-19). When you are generous to others, you lay up "treasure...as a firm foundation for the coming age"—heaven. Naturally, that generosity includes giving to the church and Christian organizations.

But what about other forms of generosity? Giving money to people when they need it or members of the family, lending your car or garden tools or other possessions, and sharing some of the yield of your garden and hobbies with friends are all forms of generosity that God honors on both sides of heaven. Even giving your children and others gifts figures in the scheme of rewards. Really, anything we give—if we give it because of our love and commitment to Christ—counts for eternity. Jesus told us that whatever we do for others, we've done for Him (Matthew 25:40).

I used to resent having to spend money on gifts for family and friends, especially when I didn't have much to give. But as I look at Paul's teaching in this passage, I don't see anything to indicate that those gifts, when given in the right spirit, don't please God and count in His eyes for eternity. Now I view everything my family gives (except paying bills—though in some cases that's an act of great grace!) as an act of goodness that wins God's approval. Such an outlook changes one's attitude tremendously. No matter what we own or earn, it's not "all ours."

Christian enterprises and leaders in business who are Christians are also responsible. God knows every heart and understands why we do what we do. If even a cup of cold water given to a child is not overlooked, how much more all other forms of giving even to the "least" of your employees?

•**Visiting orphans and widows** (James 1:27). Such a simple thing, yet it brings great reward. As a seminary student, I read this verse and decided to visit people in nursing homes. My intent was to share the gospel. But often I ended up just talking and listening to the folks I visited.

I remember one pair of rather senile ladies I befriended. On one visit they talked about how young I was and tittered about my curly hair and how they wished they had the same. When I told them my age, they couldn't believe I was all of twenty-five, so I boldly asked them how old they were. One looked at the other thoughtfully and finally said, "I don't know, honey."

But even though neither of those ladies remembered me two minutes after I left, James assures all of us that such visits are not in vain.

•**Giving to the poor, prayer, and fasting** (Matthew 6:1-18). Whole monastic orders were founded on Jesus' words in the Sermon on the Mount about almsgiving, prayer, and fasting. They did it to gain a reward from God. But we needn't join a monastic order to practice these disciplines. God remembers and promises to reward us in the next world for every prayer we pray, every gift to the poor, and every time we fast.

This is a very short list on a very long subject. But in reality any deed done which:

—was done out of love and submission to Christ

—was beneficial to others

—cost you something in time, money, or effort...

counts forever. It's as simple as that. It can range from washing a neighbor's car to giving a million dollars to a charity. It includes the simplest acts of mercy such as stopping to take a child to Sunday School, to life long dedication as a medical missionary.

Jesus gave us the principle in Matthew 10:42. It's as though Jesus took the smallest and simplest act of goodness and made it the standard for all good deeds. While the levels of reward might not be the same—as Jesus indicated in the Parable of the Talents when each servant received different rewards for different services (Luke 19:16-19)—the fact of reward remains. God will reward us for doing good, no matter how small and insignificant we might think it is now.

This doesn't mean, however, that He will reward us in this world and this time. Evangelists and preachers who proclaim a "tit for tat" idea of giving and receiving deceive their hearers. Though the Lord promises to meet our basic needs while we live on earth (Matthew 6:19-34), Scripture warns us repeatedly that our ultimate end, reward, and blessing are all far beyond this world.

HOW?

How do we begin doing those good deeds that gain heaven's rewards? Undoubtedly, you are already doing many, but there are some scriptural truths that may encourage a new look at our lives.

First, one reason God saves us is to create a people "zealous for good deeds" (Titus 2:14). Salvation isn't just to get us to heaven; God wants to make us "eager to do what is good." He desires folks who burn for nothing more than doing good to others. Imagine living in a home or working in a company where everyone looked for opportunities to do something nice, generous, helpful, or kind!

I remember a man named Joe Carson, now deceased. When I came to my first ministry as a youth pastor in Indianapolis, Indiana in 1978, the house I was to stay in was not yet ready. Joe and his wife, Ruth, opened their home to me, and I stayed with them for two weeks. I discovered in that short time that they were one couple who took hospitality seriously. They made me as comfortable as possible, cooked all my meals, and gave me complete use of the house.

After leaving and moving into my own house, I continued to observe Joe and Ruth in action. They were both retired, so Joe could be said to "have time on his hands." But he didn't waste it. When someone needed a ride somewhere, he drove up in his car, ready and willing. When the church needed work, or someone needed some help in their house, Joe offered his help with a grin and a sure hand.

To my knowledge, Joe never did anything to make a headline. He just did good, day by day, week by week, year by year. But I'm certain the Lord will one day give him a vibrant commendation and much more.

Second, the Bible equips us to do good. Second Timothy 3:16-17 tells us the Word of God is "useful for teaching, rebuking, correcting, and training in righteousness, so that the man of God may be thoroughly equipped for every good work." The ultimate goal of all Bible study, preaching, praying, and teaching is that we might be "adequate, equipped for every good work," as the NASB says.

In that passage, the word for "thoroughly equipped" is a heightened form of the word for "adequate." It might be translated, "that the man of God may be full-grown, completely able to handle every good work both wisely and maturely." Knowing the Bible trains us so that when opportunities arise, we can take full advantage of them and exploit them for the kingdom of God.

Doing good in a social sense—building housing for the homeless, sending food to a country stricken with famine, or bringing in medical help to the sick—are all "good" things, but they should be coupled with scriptural teaching and preaching. Doing good is not "good" in a lasting sense unless it contributes to the proclamation of Christ's message and person.

That doesn't mean everything we do must have a tract taped to it. Or that we should read Bible verses while we're helping the little old lady across the street. Sometimes all we can do is have the right attitude. But the Bible clearly shows that spreading the news of Jesus is what it's all about, not just doing good for good's sake.

Third, God has planned that we do good deeds. Ephesians 2:10 says we are His "workmanship, created in Christ Jesus to do good works, which God prepared in advance for us to do." In other words, our lives are like road maps which God has plotted out. At different spots on the road, He has placed opportunities to do good. As we cruise along through life, we arrive at those junctures and make our choice: Will I do good here, or pass on?

Jesus' parable of the Good Samaritan illustrates this very issue. Robbers attacked a traveler. He lay bloody and broken on the side of the road. A priest noticed him and passed on the other side. A Levite saw him and immediately crossed over to the far lane. But the Samaritan stopped, helped, and became the memorable symbol of good through the ages.

Opportunities knock all over the block. But how many of us answer?

Fourth, we are to provoke one another to love and good deeds (Hebrews 10:24-25). A primary purpose of worship and fellowship is to "spur one another on toward love and good deeds."

The writer of Hebrews urges us to become impassioned

about doing good, and angry enough about wrong to do something right about it. We can get the idea that worship in church revolves around praise, singing, prayer, and preaching. That is true. But Jesus wants us to take our worship into the streets, the highways and byways and demonstrate our love by doing good.

Much as I have racked my memory, I honestly don't remember hearing a specific sermon preached in church on simply doing good. I've heard many on how we need to get behind some issue like pro-life or the homeless. But never have I heard a pulpiteer wax eloquent about "doing good" as a lifestyle, as a daily pattern.

Yet, that's precisely what God wants us to do. He longs to raise up a people "zealous" for good deeds, who burst with a passion for helping others.

Good deeds. Nothing spectacular. Just one person helping another for God, because of their love for Jesus, and for the simple good of it.

Fifth, as we do good, God gives us grace to do more. Second Corinthians 9:8 says, "And God is able to make all grace abound to you, so that in all things, at all times, having all that you need, you will abound in every good work." The context of the passage refers to giving money, but the principle stands for any form of giving, whether it's time, words, or other gifts.

R.G. LeTourneau, who died in 1969, told *Forbes Magazine* that he loved doing two things in life. The first was designing machines and turning on the power. He made a mark in that area, designing and building many machines, among them a 200,000 pound monstrosity that cuts a 35 foot swath in the jungle, chewing up trees as thick as five feet in diameter.

But his other love—and undoutedly his first—was turning on the power of the gospel and seeing it work in people's lives. He gave over 90 percent of his income to Christian work. He spoke everywhere he could to tell others about Jesus. He founded and funded a college and engineering school dedicated both to intellectual and spiritual education. His favorite personal quote was, "It is not how much money I give to God, but how much of God's money I keep for myself."[2]

He gave and God gave him grace so he could give more. God will do the same for each of us—perhaps not in terms of money—but in a rainbow of means that together weaves a fabric of goodness so beautiful, one day the whole Christian world will stand in awe at the achievement.

Last, God is able to make our good gifts return to us. Solomon says in Ecclesiastes 11:1-2, "Cast your bread upon the waters, for after many days you will find it again. Give portions to seven, yes to eight, for you do not know what disaster may come upon the land." Nothing we do is lost. Sometimes it will return to us in this life. But if not, certainly in the one that lasts for eternity.

Two students in the first class at Stanford University in the 1890s needed money to pay their tuition and book costs. They came up with the idea of engaging Ignace Paderewski, Poland's great pianist, to perform a recital. The pianist's agent asked for a guarantee of $2000, a lot of money in those days. The boys agreed and worked hard, but they came up only with $1600.

After the concert, the students sadly presently Paderewski with the $1600 in cash and a promissory note for $400, explaining that they'd pay him back as soon as possible.

The pianist told them, "No, boys, that won't do." He tore the note in two and returned to them the other $1600. "Now take out of the $1,600 all of your expenses, and keep for each of you 10% of the balance for your work. Let me have the rest."

They did it, amazed and grateful.

Years went by. After World War I, Paderewski became premier of Poland and labored desperately to feed millions of starving people in his homeland. Only one man could help: Herbert Hoover, then in charge of the U.S. Food and Relief Bureau. After a negotiation. Hoover sent thousands of tons of food to help the great pianist.

Paderewski later traveled to Paris to thank Hoover for his help. He responded, "That's all right, Mr. Paderewski. You don't remember it, but you helped me once when I was a student at college, and I was in trouble."[3]

Have you fallen into the trap of thinking what you do amounts to little? Have some of your acts of kindness been spurned or criticized? Don't worry about it. Keep on serving the Lord. Keep on doing good. God will reward you. Don't be intimidated if the world's response is "pious" or "goody-goody" or "bleeding heart." Do good. God's keeping the records.

Do you look at the grim or nonexistent results of your work as a missionary, pastor, or teacher? Do you find yourself comparing your work to others, more famous in their fields? Keep on doing good. Don't lose heart, even if you can't see the results.

I know how often I have to remind myself of this in the face of books that go nowhere, family life that teeters on the brink of destruction, and ministries that fizzle. God sees and knows. He understands my and your situation. He's put us where we are and arranged opportunities to come our way that no one else will ever have. He expects us to keep being kind and loving and friendly and giving. It's all part of the "good works" on our heavenly resumé.

FOOTNOTES
[1] W.E. Vine, *An Expository Dictionary of New Testament Words* (Fleming H. Revell, Old Tappan, NJ, 1940), p. 164.
[2] From *Encyclopedia of 7700 Illustrations* by Paul Lee Tan (Chicago, IL, Assurance Publishers, 1979), p. 475.
[3] Cited in *Bits and Pieces* (Fairfield, NJ, The Economics Press, June 1982), pp. 14-15.

-9-
Treasure in Heaven: Sending It On Ahead

Surveys reveal that in the United States, employees steal over one percent of the Gross National Product of the U.S.—or nearly fifty billion dollars—from their own companies. This accounts for over 80% of all crime against corporations. The U.S. Chamber of Commerce estimates that three out of every ten companies that fail do so because their own employees have stolen from them.[1]

No matter how secure we try to make our possessions, someone will find a way to crack our safe, evade our computer codes, break down our triple lock doors, or muzzle our guard dogs. No form of self-protection has yet been invented that someone else hasn't invented a way to nullify.

THE ANCIENT WORLD

Jesus understood the human desire for security. He spoke of the problem we face in trying to protect our treasures in Matthew 6:19-24. He warned us that we have three problems in seeking to prevent economic disasters: moths, rust, and thieves.

In those days, people employed three basic methods to store up wealth. The first was in clothing. In II Kings 5:22, Gehazi took two changes of clothes as payment for Naaman's healing. Achan hid a "beautiful mantle of Shinar" in his tent among other things he found in the Jericho ruins (Joshua 7:21). People often hoarded their wealth in the form of clothing. They valued and invested in fabrics, even as we do today in designer gowns and name-brand suits.

But preserving clothing intact in those days posed problems. There weren't any "moth balls." Moths invaded their closets and ate holes in the precious textiles. A "beautiful mantle of Shinar" could suffer a sudden lapse into worthlessness because a moth fed on a few delicate strands one evening in August.

People saved wealth a second way by stockpiling grain and food in barns and silos. The rich farmer in Jesus' parable of the rich fool had a plan to ensure his future by building bigger and better barns for his vast holdings. They were a visible type of wealth (Luke 12:13-21).

But such stockpiling brings a terrible scourge: rats, mice, insects, and other creatures that eat up the treasure. The word "rust" which Jesus used in Matthew 6:19, can literally mean "eating," in the sense of loss of food through any process, from vermin to mildew, insect damage, and fungi.

Hard cash itself offered a third means of accumulation, either coined money, or jewelry, gold and silver objects, and precious stones. No one owned safety deposit boxes or bank vaults in those days; a person figured out his own methods. Some hid their treasures in a concealed space in the house. Others buried it in the floor or out in a field somewhere.

Of course, the problem here was thieves. Smart as the rich man might be, a smarter thief through observation or plain common sense could breach his system and heist it away. Jesus' answer to all these problems is not moth balls, pesticides, or alarm systems. Rather, He says, "Lay up treasure in heaven." No moth can fly there. No rat can sneak in through a hole. No thief can decode the combination.

WHAT IS IT?

What does it mean to lay up treasure in heaven?

Jesus uses the illustration of how we save and protect earthly wealth. He's saying that investing our money in fine clothing, stockpiling food against an insecure future, and hoarding hard cash in any form is foolish. Nothing we do can protect it permanently.

But notice what Jesus is not saying. He's not telling us to wear shabby clothing. That would contradict what He says only a few minutes later in Matthew 6:29-30. God clothes the lilies of the field beautifully; why should we think He cares less for us?

Nor is Jesus saying that we should think only about today. It's wise to plan for future problems and situations that could arise. He clearly advises us to plan ahead and think about how we'll meet the cost of things before we embark upon any project, whether it be retirement, a college education for our children, or a house (Luke 14:28-35).

Joseph became Pharaoh's right hand man because of his skill in planning and administration. Agur prayed that God would give him neither riches nor poverty, but something in between which would make him feel secure but at the same time dependent on the Lord (Proverbs 30:8-9). Jesus commended the wise servants in Matthew 25:21-23 for investing their money wisely and making more of it.

What Jesus rejects is the stockpiling of wealth in any form for the selfishness of luxurious living. In II Corinthians 8:13-14, Paul spells out the principle of why some have and others don't. "Our desire is not that others might be relieved while you are hard pressed, but that there might be equality. At the present time your plenty will supply what they need, so that in turn their plenty will supply what you need. Then there will be equality." God gives to some so they can be generous to those who have need. The reason one person might have a "mind for business" and an ability to invest wisely and make more money than others is so that he can use the wealth he makes to benefit the work of Christ in this world.

TREASURE IN HEAVEN

That brings us to the real issue of treasure in heaven. Jesus

110

says, "Don't put your treasure into expensive clothing, big houses, or huge stockpiles of food or jewels and cash you can hide away in a safe place; rather, invest it in what will last: the work of God." Whatever we choose to invest in that work is legitimate, so long as that is our motive and guiding principle.

EXAMPLES

Over the years, I've gathered a number of examples of people who have stored up treasure in heaven in unique ways.

•**Service and help ministries.** During the summer of 1988, 18 men, all white upper income professionals from Minnesota, went to Jackson, Mississippi to renovate a dilapidated house in an all black neighborhood. They came as part of Voice of Calvary, a 28-year-old ministry seeking to meet the needs of the poor. They paid their own way and even raised $10,000 for materials. Then they gave their own vacation time to work for two weeks straight on the renovation. Black and white mingled to form bonds of respect and understanding.[2]

•**Works of mercy and love.** The hospice movement is a church-related work helping people with terminal illnesses who have been discharged from the hospital because there is nothing more medicine can do.

Many churches have sponsored such works. There are some 1700 hospice programs in the U.S. today that offer assistance to families who must care for a terminally ill patient at home, as well as the patient himself.[3]

Work like this goes on day in and day out in churches across the world. Churches sponsor "Meals on Wheels" services which bring meals to the sick and shut-ins. Rescue Missions can be found in every city which seek to rescue alcoholics, the homeless, and other needy people from complete destitution.

•**A coffee service.** Recently I met Gary Berga, a businessman in Stevensville, Maryland. He owns and runs a coffee service that delivers coffee break supplies in the mid-Atlantic region of the eastern United States. All his drivers are Christians. They don't have sales meetings, he told me. "We have Bible studies." His salesmen not only sell coffee supplies, but each van is also equipped with a shelf of books they sell and use in their work of evangelism. While making a living for him- self and his employees, Gary also spreads the good news of Christ and uses his business creatively to disciple others in the faith.

•**An oculist.** Dr. Howard Hendricks has written of his oculist friend who wanted to share his faith in Christ but didn't know how. He took some training and soon began using Campus Crusade's *Four Spiritual Laws* in his work. He placed some copies in his waiting room. Frequently people came back into his office after an examination asking questions about that "fascinating little pamphlet out there."

Then the doc got a better idea. You know how an eye doctor tests your sight by having you read letters of different sizes on a wall about 20 feet away? This doctor painted the *Four Spiritual Laws* there as his wall chart. Soon he was leading people to Christ left and right.

•**Giving it all away.** Many have read the story of C.T. Studd, one of the Cambridge Seven, who dedicated his life to missions in the 1880s. He sailed for China in 1885 to serve with Hudson Taylor's China Inland Mission, giving away his inherited fortune. He founded a number of mission organizations, including the "Student Volunteer Movement," a precursor of Inter-Varsity, Campus Crusade, and Youth for Christ, and the "Heart of Africa Mission," which is presently called "The Worldwide Evangelization Crusade."

While there are few who have chosen that route in history, God promises those who give up material possessions for Him will receive them back in heaven a hundred fold (Matthew 19:29).

•**Advertising phone book.** In my area, we have a "Christian Yellow Pages," called *The Shepherd's Guide.* Doug Scheidt. Jr. founded it in 1980 because he wanted to own a business that would give him a chance to minister and also help Christians.

He envisioned a business phone book like the standard "Yellow Pages" that would advertise only businesses whose owners were committed to Jesus. The business has flourished. It provides an important service for Christians who want to do business with other Christians.

•**Ministries galore.** For nearly every need one could easily find some Christian ministry committed to reaching people with that need. Missions organizations and church planting ministries abound. While we must be careful—wise as serpents and innocent as doves—to discern bogus ministries and organizations that really do take advantage of sincere believers and use their offerings for personal gain, most ministries are run by people dedicated to serving Christ out of a genuine spirit of sacrifice and love. They live on modest incomes and work hard to do the task God has given them. Our support is not lightly regarded by them, nor by our Lord.

•**Moving into a community.** Over the years I've met people committed to friendship and lifestyle evangelism who literally move every few years because they've evangelized their community and want to work in new situations and meet more lost people. They buy a house or rent an apartment in a locale specifically to befriend the people in that area and lead them to Christ. After they've spent several years there and feel they've made the impact the Lord desired, they move on.

God leads each of us in a multitude of unique, personalized ways to use our resources for the spread of the gospel. No single ministry or service covers the market on the best or only way to serve. God's work includes a wide range of people with varying needs, interests, and desires. Thus, He raises up people who can uniquely meet those needs, whether they be rich, poor, middle class, Oriental, African, Indian, or Caucasian, speaking many languages or just one, business people, blue collar workers, or full-time ministers. For such a variety of needs, God cultivates a variety of backgrounds, abilities, talents, and desires.

SEVERAL QUESTIONS

Still, several questions come to mind.

First, is it legitimate for us to receive some benefit from what we're investing in?

Jesus counsels us to use our possessions for the work of God. Whatever resources we have that enabled us to purchase them came from Him. We're simply stewards. That we receive a benefit is no problem; it simply makes it that much more enjoyable. If a person "gets a charge out of" being a missionary in a mosquito-infested jungle, does that make his ministry somehow less spiritual? Is it only spiritual when we're gritting our teeth and fighting back the pain?

Paul told Timothy that God has given us all good things to enjoy (I Timothy 6:17). He said in the same book that even food was God's good gift; therefore, enjoy it (I Timothy 4:1-5). God knows the heart and will judge it accordingly. But when we begin judging one another, we're standing on shaky ground (James 4:11-12, 5:9; I Corinthians 4:5).

Second, do I have to give it all away? There are Scriptures that tell certain people to give everything away (such as the rich young ruler in Mark 10) and many others that counsel generosity (I Timothy 6:17-19). If all the rich people gave everything to the poor, then the poor would end up being the rich people. What happens then? Is everyone supposed to give it away the moment he gets it like a worldwide game of "hot potato"?

What the Scriptures intend, I believe, is that we avoid hoarding wealth. Saving to meet legitimate future needs is a wholly different issue. Everyone's needs are different. We cannot dictate to one another what their legitimate concerns and needs are. To run a million dollar business, a Christian businessman might need expensive clothing, a nice car, and a car phone. A missionary in Africa might choose to spend as little as possible on clothing. It's a matter of the heart, and only God knows the heart. Each of us will answer ultimately to Him for how we invested in His work.

Third, is it still treasure in heaven if I get paid for it? One issue that has always troubled me as a writer is that I get paid for how I serve the Lord—writing Christian books and speaking at retreats and seminars. For many years I felt uncomfortable about this. I thought the writer who did the church newsletter for free pleased God far more than I did in writing an article for a magazine and getting a check in the process. I suspected a speaker who came to a seminar and charged twenty dollars per attendant got his reward here on earth. But one who spoke for free or just took an offering acted spiritually. But God weighs motives and knows the heart.

Jesus told His disciples that "the worker is worthy of his wages" (Matthew 10:9-10). Paul said in I Corinthians 9:14 that those who preach the gospel should get their living from the gospel. I don't believe he meant only full-time pastors or evangelists. It must refer to anyone—part-time or full-time— who contributes to the spread of the gospel. But if their motives are rooted only in what this world offers—whether they are editors in a Christian publishing company, a secretary in a Christian organization, or the president himself—then they are fools. They're investing in the wrong things. They're wasting their time.

If our work—whatever it is—cannot qualify for financial rewards now and heavenly rewards hereafter unless it's a completely altruistic ministry where we receive nothing in this world for what we do, then no Christian should do anything except be a full-time poverty-stricken minister for Christ tramping the streets and receiving nothing in return but the most bare essentials through the charity of non-believers.

It simply is not this way. Paul knew how to get along with prosperity as well as in financial need (Philippians 4:12).

How, then, do we resolve this dilemma?

The answer is that spirituality is determined by our heart attitude and how we use what God has given us, not by neutral methodologies, any of which could find their basis in biblical principles or reasonable standards. Unless the person is abusing his use of the benefits through selfishness or greed, why should we criticize him? If he submits to a godly board of leaders, he answers to God and the governing authorities, not us. "Who are you to judge someone else's servant? To his own master he stands or falls. And he will stand, for the Lord is able to make him stand" (Romans 14:4). One day Christ will reveal all motives and give him whatever is due (I Corinthians 4:5).

Fourth, what if I'm criticized in my choices? Let's make it clear: Anyone who tries to work for Jesus Christ *will be* criticized. It matters little how great or small it is. There will be those who stand on the sidelines and throw stones. There is only one way to deal with it—listen to the criticism; separate truth from error; if you're wrong, change your ways; if you're right, or it's a matter of opinion, forget it and go on with your work. Criticism comes with the territory.

THE ISSUE

The issue ultimately comes down to a question: What are you doing to invest in the work of Christ on earth? If you're not sure, then ask, "What would I like to do? What would interest me? How can I use my God-given enjoyment of missions, or the outdoors or flute-playing to serve Him?"

Perhaps that is the very place God wants you to begin using your resources—the ones He's given to you!

FOOTNOTES
[1]Quoted in *His*, 2-83.
[2]John Prin, "The Rehabbing of 807 Pascagoula" (*Christianity Today* : November 18, 1988), pp. 12-13.
[3]Beth Spring, "A Genuinely Good Death" (*Christianity Today*: July 15, 1988), pp. 27-31.

-10-
Fruitbearing: Many Varieties, Many Possibilities

When the sower sows the Word, eventually there's a harvest. Some seed falls on hard ground and the birds of the air eat it up. Other seed lies on the rocky soil which has no depth. Though the seed springs up, when the sun comes out it dries up and goes fruitless. Still other seed sinks into the weedy soil. It makes a good start, but eventually the weeds choke it out.

But the seed that germinates in the "good soil" is what it's all about. That seed grows into a fine stalk of corn or wheat or even a whole fig, olive, apple or orange tree. When the harvest comes, it fills the baskets and the master goes off to market with joy in his heart.

The Bible speaks of several kinds of fruit the Christian can and should bear in his life. Moreover, through bearing fruit, we attract the hungry to our Master.

DIFFERENT BRANDS

There are seven varieties of fruit in Scripture, all of which should find a proper branch in our spiritual lives.

•**Character and holiness** (Galatians 5:22-23). Spiritual fruit is undoubtedly the most important fruit we can bear in our lives. It's the key to all the rest. The qualities of love, joy, peace, patience, kindness, goodness, faithfulness, gentleness, and

117

self-control govern how we relate to ourselves, how we respond to others, and how we revere the Lord. We'll discuss this in the next chapter.

•**Sowing the Word and reaping souls** (Proverbs 11:30-31; Matthew 13:8). God desires that we win others to His Son. The process of salvation is largely one soul passing on the Good News to another. Whether we hear through a book, a magazine, a face to face talk, a message in a church or rally, a tract, or some other means, it's almost always one person telling another about who Jesus is, what He did, and how to know Him.

Fruitbearing is not just reaping souls; it's more sowing than anything else (I Corinthians 3:6-7). While one may reap a soul by actually bringing him to the decision to trust Christ, twenty or a hundred people may have been involved in the process of sowing, planting, and nurturing that seed.

•**Personal commitment to Christ** (Matthew 7:15-20). There is such a thing as "fruit inspection." We tell a false prophet or teacher by observing his fruit. What is he producing? Works, colleges, books, and churches that are a monument to himself—or that glorify Christ? Whom does he reflect? Good fruit results from rejoicing in the Fruitgiver. Bad fruit calls attention to itself. Ministers and leaders in recent days have used their names, positions, power, and prestige for self-gain and self-exaltation. Scandals resulted and have torn some major ministries to confetti.

James Calvert (1813-1892) was born in Pickering, England. Saved at the age of 18, he went to Hoxton Theological Seminary for training in missions. An urgent call to the Fiji Islands led him to cut short his studies and head out with two other men to work among the cannibals. As he stood aboard the ship, the captain tried to stop him. He said, "You will lose your life and the lives of those with you if you go among such savages." Calvert replied, "We died before we came here."

Over the next quarter century, a remarkable transformation happened among the tribesmen of those islands. Hundreds were saved. Calvert's fruit was commitment and service to Christ. That earnest labor bore more fruit in character and souls won to the cross.

Years later, an English earl visited the Fiji Islands. He was an infidel and he critically remarked to one of the converted chieftains, "You're a great leader, but it's a pity you've been taken in by those foreign missionaries. No one believes the Bible anymore. People are tired of the threadbare story of Christ dying on a cross for the sins of mankind. They know better now. I'm sorry you've been so foolish as to accept their story."

The old chief answered with flashing eyes, "See that great rock over there? On it we smashed the heads of our victims. Notice the furnace next to it. In that oven we formerly roasted the bodies of our enemies. If it hadn't been for those good missionaries and the love of Jesus that changed us from cannibals into Christians, you'd never leave this place alive! You'd better thank the Lord for the gospel; otherwise we'd already be feasting on you. If it weren't for the Bible and its salvation message, you'd now be our supper!"

Calvert's commitment not only led to fruit, but to converts who would continue the legacy.

•**Making wrongs right** (Matthew 3:8; Acts 26:20). One of the first fruits of true Christian living is a turning away from the old life and a desire to make wrong deeds right, or at least make apology, reparation, and restoration. John the Baptist told the Pharisees, "Produce fruit in keeping with repentance" (Matthew 3:8).

One young man I know came to Christ out of a highly hedonistic culture where drugs, sex, and alcohol were the flames of the game. He realized how he had abused relationships, especially with women. Having turned to Christ, he went to each of them to offer a sincere apology. Some were appalled. Others said he'd done no wrong. Several argued with him that he had gone off the deep end. But one had become a Christian and accepted his apology, saying, "We can't turn back the past, but we can make a better future."

Other Christians have made reparation for thefts, lies, violent acts. It's all part of the process of bearing true fruit. True fruit feeds not only the souls of those who are hungry, but our own soul as well.

•**Righteousness** (Philippians 1:11). As we grow in righteousness we bear a fragrant fruit in God's eyes. Character is what we are, but righteousness pictures how we act toward the world, God, and others. Doing justice and choosing the right way counts in God's eyes. Every time we choose to do what's right out of love for the Lord and a desire to obey Him, we please Him. Undoubtedly, such acts win God's approval and delight.

Righteousness is simply doing what is right in God's eyes. That guarantees His support and pleasure.

•**Giving** (Philippians 4:17). Giving money and resources to the work of Christ is a form of fruitbearing, too. Everything we give in the name of Christ is treasure stored in heaven; it is fruit that lasts into eternity.

•**Thanksgiving and praise** (Hebrews 13:15). The fruit of our lips—thanksgiving, praise, rejoicing, worship of God, and witnessing of Christ—lasts forever. Whenever we overflow with thanks from a heart of love, God remembers. Revelation 8:3-4 speaks of our prayers being like incense before the throne of heaven. We are to enter His gates "with thanksgiving and his courts with praise" (Psalm 100:4). Do you enter His presence with thanksgiving and praise?

THE MARVEL

Bearing fruit is a great joy in the Christian life. But the greatest marvel is the fact that as we bear fruit, God nurtures us so that we can bear more. God constantly prunes the branches of those who bear fruit so that they can bear more (John 15:2).

I have a friend who used to own a vineyard. He gave it up because it was so much work cutting back the vines. It astonished me how meticulously he worked those vines. He pored over every shoot with gentle, probing eyes and fingers. He told me that too many grapes siphoned off the best juices. He wanted not only to produce more grapes, but better, more succulent, luscious, and juicy grapes—in short, the best.

I have often wondered why some Christians seem to overflow with productive Christian lives while others languish and never seem to get anywhere. I believe it's the principle of abiding and pruning. As we walk with Christ, we begin to bear fruit. As we bear fruit, the Spirit works in us, pruning away undesirable shoots and branches. Gradually, we learn that singleminded devotion which capitalizes on the things we do best and yields the fruit that lasts.

BECOMING MORE FRUITFUL

How, then, do you become more fruitful? Scripture gives us a number of principles.

First, by giving your life in obedience to Christ. In John 12:24-25, Jesus speaks of the seed that falls into the soil and dies. But once it dies, it begins to bear fruit.

The person who commits his life to Christ and dies to whatever earthly ambitions and lofty goals he might have, submitting instead to the plan of God, bears more and more fruit in his life. God's plan often includes the very ambitions we might have had before. Sometimes it doesn't. But whichever way it goes, real fruit only comes through real submission.

Second, by knowing, meditating on, and applying God's Word to your life. Psalm 1 portrays the life of the person who refuses the counsel of the ungodly and heeds the law of God, meditating on it and living it out day by day. "He is like a tree planted by streams of water, which yields its fruit in season" (Psalm 1:3).

Third, by depending on Christ. Our abilities have only one Source. In John 15:5, Jesus said, "Apart from me you can do nothing." How much clearer can He make it?

Finally, submitting to His efforts to prune us. That process of pruning sometimes hurts. It calls for trial, difficulty, and harsh circumstances. God may send such problems into our lives to teach us to become more effective fruitbearers, or to shape us in a different direction.

The Lord uses the kinds of discipline that we'd often like to avoid to enable us to bear fruit. Once we learn one lesson, He teaches us another. As we develop particular areas of strength, He strengthens us in it. It's not only the person who learns the most lessons who can bear the most fruit in the kingdom of God; it's also the one who understands their limits, too.

A woman in my church with cerebral palsy often stunned us with her words of praise and love. Confined to a wheelchair, her arms twisted in front of her, she often joked that she spoke "Cepanses"—the sometimes fractured language of people with her handicap. She always had encouraging words for those who spoke to her. Her gift, I believe, was exhortation. In one sharing service, she told us of her growth and love for the Lord, and concluded, "Knowing the Lord makes me feel like a butterfly." God limited her physically, but she used it for His glory and praise.

The concentrated stream of light through a magnifying glass sets wood aflame. God shines His light on us and through us. But like a magnifying glass, though He pours much into us, He desires that only a concentrated stream come out so we can set the world on fire. By concentrating our efforts, we actually bear far more fruit than if we try to accomplish too much and end up with nothing that lasts.

-11-

How Important Is Personal Character Now When We'll End Up Perfect Anyway?

"God's going to make me perfect. So why worry what I'm like now?"

So said one student as we explored the biblical realities of rewards and our future in heaven. Indeed, in some ways it makes sense. No matter how developed we are in holiness and faith, in the "twinkling of an eye" we will be made perfect. That perfection launches us light years ahead of anything we could accomplish now. If we compare perfection to a hundred miles and the most we can travel in this life is two inches, why try? Why not just wait for that moment when we'll be whisked through the whole distance without batting an eye?

SPACESHIPS

Max Rice uses an interesting illustration in his book, *Your Rewards In Heaven*. Suppose this King has an important task to fulfill. He builds a fleet of amazing spaceships to achieve his goals. These spaceships zoom through space at the speed of light. He equips them with instruments and technology that can do virtually anything—turn on a dime, destroy whole galaxies at the push of a button, create their own food and resources, establish space stations, carry monumental payloads, dig out valuable ore and jewels from other planets. The commander in charge of each spaceship will possess marvelous powers to do battle, transform, create, and destroy.

But how could the King be sure that his chosen commanders wouldn't use the spaceships for their own ends, or even rankly evil purposes?

That's where stage one of the plan comes into effect. In order to see who will use his spaceships wisely and faithfully, the King begins a program in which he tests every commander on much smaller and limited spacecraft. He prints an instruction manual that tutors the pilot about everything he needs to know to fly effectively. Each commander thus displays what he will do in a free-choice-rich environment. In the process, he will reveal his true concerns and what matters to him or her. On the basis of how they perform in the limited environment, the King then decides how and whether he will employ them on board the super spaceships.[1]

THE REALITY

In a sense, that is precisely what God is doing in our world today. He has prepared a potent, intellectually-unlimited, emotionally-rich spaceship called "the new heavens and the new earth." Aboard this ship, every resident will possess monumental, eternal, and indestructible powers and abilities. They will wield epoch-making authority. They will rule over the universe with an undefeatable hand. The question is, how can God responsibly and reasonably allow anyone to live in that place?

What if a Hitler received those powers? What havoc might he wreak? What if Charles Manson or Saddam Hussein suddenly became master of unlimited, eternal, and indestructible powers? How would the rest of us fare in such an environment?

The truth is that the new heavens and the new earth—if

anyone anywhere from any time could gain access—would become a galactic battleground that would put any sci-fi scenario to shame.

To prevent that possibility, God is using the present earth as a training and testing ground to see who will be loyal to Him, and who won't. He selects only those who exercise faith in Christ for service above. He disqualifies those without faith.

But beyond that, a number of other tests must follow once someone has demonstrated faith. Going back to the spaceship illustration, what if some pilots, while they trust the Commander, prefer doing it "their way" instead of as the instruction manual shows? What if others, while committed to the Commander, do not study the guidelines thoroughly enough to fly well? What if still others choose to discard the Commander's work and whiz off on their own pleasure cruises? And what if some pilots neglect their spaceships and end up crashing them, or even corrupting the planets they visit?

The point is that God tests us now for precisely these purposes. While we can't know what He plans for each of us in heaven, the training and testing we go through now must have some eternal purpose. This is why growing in character is so critical. God is preparing us for the work and world of eternity.

Someone has said, "Character is what a man is when no one else is looking." True. But beyond that, integrity and heart character involve what God sees in us. When we stand before Him, He will reveal our true character to all creation, and that will determine what role we have in heaven.

WHAT THE BIBLE SAYS ABOUT CHARACTER
Consider some of the things the Bible says about character.

•**We are commanded to be holy.** First Peter 1:16 says, "Be holy, because I am holy."

•**God has a purpose for our character development.** Paul says in II Timothy 2:21: "If a man cleanses himself from the latter [ignoble purposes], he will be an instrument for noble purposes, made holy, useful to the Master and prepared to do any good work."

•**A godly life reflects joy and peace.** The fruit of the Spirit listed in Galatians 5:22-23 imparts a vivid picture of the life of holiness. A person who overflows with love, joy, peace, patience, kindness, goodness, faithfulness, gentleness, and self-control is equipped to serve God wholeheartedly in the here—and the hereafter.

•**Sin enslaves; the Word frees.** We attain true freedom only through knowing God's Word and doing it. Jesus said in John 8:31-32, "If you hold to my teaching you are really my disciples. Then you will know the truth, and the truth will set you free."

•**Only spiritual character can please God.** Paul advised us in Romans 8:6-8, "The mind of sinful man is death, but the mind controlled by the Spirit is life and peace; the sinful mind is hostile to God. It does not submit to God's law, nor can it do so. Those controlled by the sinful nature cannot please God."

•**God gives the crown of righteousness to those who finish the race.** Paul states this in II Timothy 4:8 and in I Corinthians 9:24-27. While we're not altogether sure what this crown entails, clearly it's something Paul prized.

HOW TO GROW IN CHARACTER

How then do you grow in character? Many regimens have been proposed, and everyone has his own little diagram of how to grow in grace. But four elements suffice.

1. Through worship of God through Jesus Christ. Peter tells us to "grow in the grace and knowledge of our Lord and Savior Jesus Christ" in II Peter 3:18. We grow primarily through grace—in obedience—and knowledge of Jesus.

Worship transforms the person who worships. Have you ever found yourself in the presence of someone who exudes grace and godliness? Such people exert a powerful influence.

In their presence, we speak respectfully, honestly, directly. We act in a different way when they're around.

Recently, I had an opportunity to visit and talk with a famous minister whose words and works have influenced me by tape and book for years. Although at first I felt shy and timid in his presence, his kind manner set me at ease. Yet, while I talked affably with him, I restrained myself from saying or doing things that might bring me shame. Afterward, I realized that I should act and treat all people as I had treated that man—with respect, admiration, gentility.

In the same way, I see the application to worship. The more we live and walk in the presence of God, the more time we spend in prayer, conscious of His nearness, the more we become like Him and the more awe and reverence we feel. People know when we've "been with Jesus" (Acts 4:13).

Brother Lawrence, the 17th century monk who wrote the book, *The Practice of the Presence of God*, said, "The end we ought to propose to ourselves is to become, in this life, the most perfect worshipers of God we can possibly be, as we hope to be through eternity." Worship and knowledge of the Lord transfuses and transforms us.

2. Through practice of the Word of God. Hebrews 5:13-14 tells us that the Spirit trains our senses to discern good and evil through "practice."

The only way to grow in holiness—to abandon evil and saturate our lives with good—is simply practicing the actions and motives of holiness. That requires the application of the Word of God consistently and rigorously to our circumstances. Knowledge of the facts is not enough, although that's important. Memorizing the Word soaks our minds with truth; but merely knowing what the Bible says is minor compared to acting on what it commands. Being able to spout five points about the deity of Christ might awe some. But living them delights the Lord.

3. Through fellowship with other Christians. Real fellowship stimulates growth. I don't mean the cookies and coffee social gatherings that many call "fellowship." Real fellowship involves what Hebrews 10:24-25 calls spurring "one another on toward love and good deeds." In true Christian *koinonia*, we engage in such interpersonal activities as encouragement, mutual honor, comfort, exhortation, confrontation, restoration, confession of sin, devotion, instruction, and sacrificial love. In real fellowship we develop and use our spiritual gifts. We meet to build up one another and help one another grow in character and grace.

During World War II, German experimenters concluded that the most successful method in cracking prisoners was through placing them in solitary confinement. After a few days alone in a tiny cell, many men would come out willing to tell all, if only they could be joined again with others.

We should not expect Christian fellowship to be all rhyme and roses. Instead, real fellowship sometimes bites and barks. It forces us to consider whether our beliefs and convictions are sound.

4. Through witness and discipleship. God wants us to tell the Good News for more reasons than just to spread the Word. We have to consider what witnessing and discipleship do to the witnesser!

Tangling with an unbeliever usually enhances and stretches one's faith. The challenge of mind meeting mind and facing the hard questions pushes us to search, work, sweat, and bleed in the pursuit of truth. On occasion, secular opinion has so stymied me that I've been forced to research the issue just to find out if what I believed was true.

On another front, witnessing compels us to examine our own character and reputation. How can we go out and tell others to believe something when they could legitimately point out flaws in our behavior? Witnessing is one of the faith's surest ways to get us to clean up our lives!

While working in a full-time secular job, I found myself

struggling to witness at one point. I prayed about it and finally realized I didn't feel comfortable witnessing because the quality of my work was deficient. How could I go tell someone who was doing a better job than me how to get his life together? I had to get my work up to snuff just so I could give a credible witness.

Witnessing also teaches us about taking a stand. Students at Marquette University once razzed a political candidate running for president. He spoke frequently of his faith in Christ. A student challenged him, "Tell us about your relationship with God." Snickers and catcalls cut the air. But the candidate replied, "I am a devout Christian. The presence of my belief in Jesus Christ is the most important thing in my life. I am not ashamed of it. In the last ten years I have had a most intimate relationship with God through Jesus Christ. It is a matter of privacy; but also a matter of which I am not ashamed. I hope in my decisions as President I will be guided by the principles in which I believe." They tore him to pieces. But he stood firm. His name was Jimmy Carter.

THE SPIRIT DOES IT

Those kinds of stories thrill me. They push me to complete the work God has given me. They remind me that growing in character isn't a horrible by-product of accepting Christ; rather, it's the ultimate meaning of life—to become like Him in person and outlook and action.

Do you ever feel growth and holiness are not worth it? That they're too hard and you should give up? That's only the devil talking, trying to force you into a black hole of discouragement. Holiness, character, and a godly life are worth the effort. Maybe you're not seeing the results you'd like to see right now, but God looks at it differently. Our sufferings produce "an eternal glory that far outweighs them all" (II Corinthians 4:17). Our present troubles are not "worthy comparing with the glory that will be revealed in us" (Romans 8:18).

Pressure. Discipline. Faith. God is with us every step. Even when all seems lost, we are achieving an overwhelming victory through Him who loves us (Romans 8:19-23) and is with us always, even to the very end of the age (Matthew 28:20).

FOOTNOTES
[1]Max Rice, *Your Rewards in Heaven* (Accent Publications, Denver, CO, 1981), pp. 53-55. Used with permission.

-12-
A Little Thing Like Obeying—Is That Important?

Merely knowing the Word of God matters little if we don't obey it. The Pharisees memorized much of the Old Testament. Yet, all that their labor in the texts accomplished was to plate on a thicker coating of lovelessness, self-righteousness, and loathing of others. They knew the truth; they didn't obey it.

Philippians 2:5-8 offers us one of the greatest anthems of praise about the mission and character of Jesus. "Your attitude should be the same as that of Christ Jesus: who, being in very nature God, did not consider equality with God something to be grasped, but made himself nothing, taking the very nature of a servant, being made in human likeness. And being found in appearance as a man, he humbled himself and became obedient to death—even death on a cross!"

That's true obedience. Not many Christians take it to that limit. We obey to the point of satisfaction, then we slack off. Or we obey so long as we see results; but when the results stop, we stop. Or, we obey even when it hurts; but if it hurts too much, we give up.

Obedience counts in the eyes of God. But what good is it? Is obedience something God will reward us for? Absolutely. Notice the passage that follows Philippians 2:5-8: "Therefore God exalted him to the highest place...."

God glorified Christ for His obedience. Other passages tell us: "Humble yourselves before the Lord, and he will lift you up" (James 4:10). "Humble yourselves, therefore, under God's mighty hand, that he may lift you up in due time" (I Peter 5:6-7). When we humble ourselves in the presence of God, we submit to Him; we obey.

WHAT THE BIBLE SAYS

So what does the Bible say about obedience?

First, God puts a premium on obedience. In I Samuel 15, King Saul disobeyed the Lord's express command to destroy the Amalekites. Saul left the best of the animals and the king alive. When Samuel confronted Saul, he became enraged. He claimed that they'd left the animals alive so they could sacrifice them to the Lord (verse 15). Samuel wasn't impressed. He informed Saul that God expected obedience to His commands, not Saul's creative variations on the theme, which were evil excuses in a bad disguise.

God regards obedience as paramount, especially among those in positions of leadership. If the subjects see that the king or president or chief executive officer takes God's words and commands lightly, they will also.

Saul argued with Samuel, trying first to blame the soldiers, and then to say they intended to sacrifice the animals to God. Saul was trying desperately to get out of a rough spot by making up some reasonable reasons for his disobedience.

Nonetheless, Samuel replied in I Samuel 15:22-23, "Does the Lord delight in burnt offerings and sacrifices as much as in obeying the voice of the Lord? To obey is better than sacrifice, and to heed is better than the fat of rams. For rebellion is like the sin of divination, and arrogance like the evil of idolatry."

God demands plain, unblinking obedience to His Word, not any amount of creativity, human pragmatism, inventiveness, or personal sacrifice that has nothing to do with His plan. How often do we obey the Lord's Word to the letter or add our own variations that offer supposedly "better" ways of doing the same thing?

Husbands and wives divorce today because of "irreconcilable differences," or "unsolvable problems." Sometimes these people say, "God has given me peace about it." And, "I feel it's right." Unfortunately, that thinking fails to reckon with the Word of God. The Lord simply does not contradict Himself (Malachi 2:16; Ecclesiastes 5:2-5).

We all like to bring our own interpretations and ideas to God's themes. But in most cases, the Bible speaks clearly and without complexity. There may be times in our lives when we honestly do not know or understand what a text means, or what God wants us to do. But usually, the problem is that we simply don't want to do as He says, so we find some way around it as Saul tried to do.

God removed Saul as king for his disobedience. God also forbade Moses from going into the Promised Land because he disobeyed (Numbers 20:12). Nadab and Abihu suffered instant death for bringing "unauthorized fire" to the Lord in the temple (Numbers 3:4). The congregation stoned Achan and his whole family for taking articles God told them to leave alone at the destruction of Jericho (Joshua 7:10-26). While God does not always punish immediately, it's obvious that disobedience incurs His wrath.

Second, God loathes ritual apart from heart obedience (Isaiah 1:11-17, 29:13-14; Micah 6:6-8). True obedience involves an obedient heart attitude as well as physical actions. Doing something for show, or even doing it with no real heart commitment, is empty, even blasphemous. God warned Israel repeatedly in the Old Testament to get their hearts right before Him. He wanted a relationship characterized by love and faith, not ritual permeated with resentment and loathing.

This applies to how we interact in church worship, how we practice intimacy with God, and why we do what we do. I think there is much to be said for the person who follows through and obeys, even though he may feel tired, unhappy, "out of it," or "not into it."

Perhaps you've had this experience. An upsetting weekend hangs behind you. Things went poorly. You wish you could sleep in Sunday morning. But you go to church anyway, perhaps even with a lingering desire to crawl back into that bed. Once at church, though you admit your feelings, you simply can't get up a head of joy about the service. You mouth the hymns. You plunk your envelope into the offering. You try to follow the sermon. But all along, you fight a fierce headache, you wish it would just be over, and you recognize deep down that God probably wasn't very pleased with your performance today.

Now what happens? Is that service written off? Will the recording angel write—"bad attitude in worship on March 24"?

Changing creatures that we are, I'm convinced that God honors our obedience even when we have mixed feelings. He knows our frame and foibles. I don't think He discounts our obedience just because we're tired or feeling lousy or not doing it with a hop, skip, and a jump. Jesus went to the cross—but He still asked the Father to remove the cup from Him. Did He have the wrong attitude? Does obedience mean we do everything with a smile and loud, "Praise the Lord!"?

No! Motives are important. But feelings are a different matter altogether. Perhaps obeying even when we don't "feel" like it is one of the highest forms of obedience of all. Then we're doing it out of pure love and reverence for God.

Third, even Christ had to learn obedience. Hebrews 5:8 says, "Although he was a son, he learned obedience form what he suffered." God understands us right through to the heart.

When we obey in the midst of pain and suffering, we discover the core of what pleases God. It's easy to obey when you "want to" or when what you're doing is fun and exhilarating. But what about when it's sheer torture? What about when every choice invites a nail in your wrists?

That's when obedience becomes a form of worship. Sticking with the program even when everything in you screams, "Quit! Give up! It's not worth it!" wafts a fragrant aroma into God's nostrils. Obeying is worth it because God says it's worth it.

Joseph P. Lash writes in his book, *Helen and Teacher* about the life of Anne Sullivan, Helen Keller's first teacher. Early on, Anne realized she had to remove Helen from her home environment. It had become too easy for her to disobey everyone. She had learned some potent manipulative habits. But Anne wrote of the experience, "I saw clearly that it was useless to try to teach her language or anything else until she learned to obey me. I have thought about it a great deal, and the more I think the more certain I am that obedience is the gate through which knowledge, yes, and love, too, enter the mind of a child."[1]

Similarly, our Christian growth depends on how well we learn the principles of obedience to Christ!

Fourth, God will discipline us to teach us to obey. Hebrews 12:1-13 records several trenchant truths about God's discipline. God not only desires our obedience, but He will make sure we learn to obey. Obedience is so important to Him that He will do all it takes to bring us to that place of obedience and truth.

Deuteronomy 32:10-11 offers a convicting word on this truth. Moses writes, "He shielded him and cared for him; he guarded him as the apple of his eye, like an eagle that stirs up its nest and hovers over its young, that spreads its wings to catch them and carries them on its pinions." Moses spoke of something he had observed in the wilderness—the way an eagle trains its young to fly. Eagles in that region build their nests high in the crags and trees. In the bottom of the nest, they lay a groundwork of prickers, sticks, and sharp stones. They cover this with feathers, skins, and leaves, all kinds of soft articles to create a warm, inviting nest.

But when the baby eagle reaches flying age, the parent rips the bottom out, exposing all the sharp, uncomfortable sticks

135

and thorns. This is what Moses meant by "stirring up the nest." The little eagle leaps for the edge, not knowing that his parents want him to fly. He looks down over the edge and spins back, dizzy and afraid. He hooks his claws to the top edge like a vice.

His parents, though, are determined. They fly at him, "hover over him," as the text says, and pummel him with their wings. He loses his grip, falls back, then forward, and suddenly he's over the edge, plummeting to the ground. As he flails at the air trying to fly, his father "spreads his wings to catch him" and whooshes under him at the last death-defying second, then carries him on his back (his "pinions") to safety. They repeat the process until the eaglet learns to fly.

This shows perfectly the process of growth and obedience in the life of the Christian. God often "stirs up our nest" with trouble and difficulty to get us to grow and follow Him. He lets us flutter over the edge and career toward disaster, then rescues us at the last moment. In the process, we learn we can trust Him to guard us even as we struggle to test our real wings.

God's discipline has a purpose—glory, His—and growth, ours. But sometimes that discipline burns us to the bone.

Joni Eareckson Tada has written extensively about her experiences as a quadriplegic and what brought her to unwavering convictions about God's goodness, love, and power to order everything in life for our good. She recorded her early struggles in her best-selling book, *Joni*. During her transition from a life-loving, exuberant teenager to a woman confined to a wheelchair with little control over her body or environment, she wept and battled anger, bitterness, doubt, and despair daily. But God enlisted a number of caring people who helped mold her thinking so that she could accept her injuries as the sovereign will of a wise, loving, and omnipotent God. She came to believe that He does work all things for good and that nothing happened to her which He didn't plan beforehand.

She emerged a confident, committed disciple who began speaking to crowds and leading hundreds to Christ. In the epilogue of that book, Joni shares her thoughts as she waited to speak at a Youth for Christ rally of over 2,000 teenagers. She reminisces through her many experiences. But at one point, she says, "I'm really thankful He did something to get my attention and change me."

Joni revealed earlier that this attitude of thanksgiving was a hard lesson. In the beginning she couldn't give thanks. But there came a day when she knew God's Word commanded it, and she obeyed. She gave thanks because He said to, even though she didn't feel thankful. In time, though, her obedience produced a strange afterglow. She soon learned to give thanks and live out His commands with genuine feeling. Her verbal thanks was matched by a radiance in the heart.

God taught her the ultimate fruit of obedience: joy.[2]

Sometimes He does have to put us on our backs to get our attention. People like Catherine Marshall, Chuck Colson, John MacArthur, and Leighton Ford have attested to that fact. But He does it out of love. And He does it so that we can soar, not sit, simmer, and stare.

Every form of obedience counts in God's eyes. The wife who remains with her husband through alcoholism, bitterness, or even lovelessness out of the conviction that divorce is wrong, honors the Lord. The teenager who honors his parents even though they lash out and mistreat him, wins the Lord's favor. The salesman who loses sales because he won't bribe or perk his customers glorifies Christ.

Obedience in big ways and small ways matters now, and in eternity. If you feel as though your obedience to God's will has brought only difficulty and trial into your life, take heart. Paul knew the feeling well. But he said, "I consider that our present sufferings are not worth comparing with the glory that will be revealed in us" (Romans 8:18).

Feeling like tears, toil, uselessness, and sweat? Think "glory!" That's what obedience to Christ wins for all eternity!

FOOTNOTES

[1]Joseph P. Lash, *Helen and Teacher* (Delacorte Press, New York, NY, 1980), p. 52.

[2]Joni Eareckson, *Joni* (Zondervan, Grand Rapids, MI, 1976), p. 226.

-13-
I Thought Stewardship Was Keeping My Car In Shape!

A friend of mine treats his possessions with utmost care. He keeps his lawn trimmed and neat, watering it every morning. I frequently see him on his roof fixing shingles and hear him banging away tiling a floor. He washes both cars once a week. One day I asked him why he washes his cars so often. He replied, "Because I want to keep them in good shape. I don't want to lose money on them."

A pastor I know has a name for people who get up early Sunday morning to labor on their lawn all day instead of going to church: "Lawn-worshipers!"

But another pastor-friend experienced severe rejection when he moved into a new community. He found out why from a neighbor: "The previous owner was a minister, and he let his lawn grow a foot tall before he cut it. He made our community look bad." This man obviously was no "grass-worshiper!" But on the other hand, he hurt his testimony by failing to maintain basic standards.

So how much time and effort should we as Christians put into the stewardship of our possessions? Does washing the car or trimming the lawn please God, or is it a peripheral we don't need to worry about?

Stewardship ranks high both as a Christian principle and a

reason for which God gives rewards. All God's gifts—from intellect and physical prowess to the screwdrivers in your cellar tool shop—are only on loan from God to you. We cannot "possess" them beyond our short sojourn in this world. The Lord regards us as caretakers, stewards, servants, and employees in His work force. Ultimately, everything in life, viewed from a Christian perspective, stands as a temporary grant from God. To paraphrase Job, "God can give, and God can take away—anytime He wants!" Sometimes He removes a possession by destruction, such as losing your house in a flood. Sometimes He plucks it away through a financial loss, or an accident—such as going blind. Sometimes He detaches us away from it—through a move, through sickness, through death.

Scripture teaches repeatedly that we are aliens and strangers on this planet. We own nothing. Naked we came into the world, and naked we leave it. We're just passing through. While we're here, though, God entrusts to us certain riches. How we use those resources determines the kind of reward we receive in heaven.

STEWARDS OF WHAT?

Of what, then, does the Bible say we are to be stewards?

•**Our spiritual gifts and abilities** (I Peter 4:10, II Timothy 1:6-7, I Corinthians 7:7). Every Christian possesses certain spiritual gifts and abilities. They are spiritual in that they flow from our spirits to minister to the spirits of others. These gifts enable us to minister to people in the very depths of who they are. Thus, a spiritual gift is more than just a talent for making floral displays or playing the piano. It's a supernatural ability to touch a person at the point of his relationship with God.

For instance, a non-Christian doctor might have a "gift" for healing people. However, the Christian doctor, while competent at physical healing, goes a step further: people who come to him find solace, hope, and joy. Spiritual gifts always point the recipient to God, either directly or indirectly.

140

•**Material possessions** (Luke 19:12-27, 12:42-48). Every material thing we own is a temporary gift of God. We don't simply hold it because we had the finesse or acumen to make the money to buy it; no, it's on loan from God. He expects us to take care of it with that view in mind.

One man I know took Christian stewardship to heart. He realized that his possessions—his house, stereo, bank account, car, etc.—were all loans. God gave them to him to take care of for the time being. This man found it a particularly comforting truth when he had an auto accident that was not his fault. As he viewed the damage and the crumpled fender, he prayed, "Well, God, if that's the way you want to treat *your* car, it's all right by me!"

That may be taking it a little far, but that's precisely the way God wants to view possessions.

On the other hand, God entrusts us with material items and expects us to take care of them. Burning up a car engine because we allowed the oil level to get too low is unfaithful stewardship. Neglect of property, failing to repair your house when it needs it, and abusing things as mundane as stereo or video equipment invites discipline. Treating His gifts with disrespect shows Him disrespect.

The principle, though, of taking good care of our possessions—from our budget to our body—demonstrates faith, obedience, and respect toward God. You don't have to be a grass-worshiper to keep your lawn trimmed and attractive. It's just possible that some Christians will receive high commendation from the Lord for their special care of His gifts and the testimony that accompanies it.

•**The people under our care** (Hebrews 13:17, I Peter 5:5, I Timothy 5:8). Anyone in a position of leadership, from an elementary school teacher to a Sunday School teacher, from a parent to the president of the United States, has people entrusted to his care. Those people belong to God. How we treat, lead, and develop those people is a matter of acute concern to the Father.

141

Every level of "people care"—from working in a nursing home to heading a family to running an arm of the government or a corporation—will be scrutinized by our heavenly Father.

That means that being a good steward as a parent or spouse is a high priority. Failure here spells real failure in God's eyes. The Lord certainly doesn't want us to alienate our families. We can't be responsible for their decisions to follow Christ, but we are responsible for such things as the neglect, abuse, and hypocrisy that move them to reject our Lord.

On the other hand, if God will reward us for giving a cup of cold water to a child, how many cups of water, plates of beans, and gifts of love should we offer our own children out of love for Him and them?

•**God's Word and mysteries** (I Corinthians 4:1-2; I Timothy 6:17-20). Every Christian is a steward of the "mysteries of God." One of the chief mysteries is "Christ in you, the hope of glory" (Colossians 1:27). The fact that God dwells in each believer is a profound truth, but also a mystery no one knew about until God chose to reveal it through the apostles in the first century.

There are other mysteries including Christ Himself (Colossians 1:9-20), the final redemption of Israel (Romans 11:25), the inspiration of Scripture (I Corinthians 2:7-10), the rapture and our transformation from the earthly to the heavenly (I Corinthians 15:51-54), the fullness of the times (Ephesians 1:9-10), the inclusion of Gentiles in the body of Christ (Ephesians 3:4-6), faith in Christ (I Timothy 3:9), godliness (I Timothy 3:16), and the last days of the world (Revelation 10:7).

Knowing about these truths is a sacred trust. Paul told Timothy to "guard the good deposit" which he had been given (II Timothy 1:14). Not only must we tell others what we know, but we also must guard those truths from dilution, addition, and misuse. If a Christian knows a speaker is teaching rank heresy, we're responsible to tell him precisely that. If he laughs at us or the Scriptures we show them, they do so to their own peril.

Every Christian has been given stewardship of the greatest truths of the universe: the reality of God, the hope of redemption, and the way to salvation. Failure to give that message to people without knowledge and hope is criminal. That does not mean we must buttonhole every person we pass in a corridor. But it does call for an honest effort to reach our neighbors, friends, and relatives with the "good news."

As stewards of a profound and life-transforming mystery, God will call us to account for how well we handled that responsibility.

•**Our ministries** (I Corinthians 9:17; I Peter 4:10; II Timothy 1:8-10). No two Christians exhibit the same gifts and ministry. But every Christian has *some* ministry. A "minister" is a servant. His service speaks of the way he serves God and God's people.

When we find our service niche, the Lord desires that we work at it with excellence, perseverance, and consistency. Solomon said it another way, "Whatever your hand finds to do, do it with all your might" (Ecclesiastes 9:10).

In the area of ministry, singlemindedness is important. It's better to do one ministry well than two or more poorly. It's better to teach a class of five with excellence and excitement than a class of five hundred with carelessness and lack of concern.

We may not make a mark that shakes today's world, but any ministry which helps, loves, gives, and teaches Jesus Christ makes quakes in the world to come.

•**Our life's work** (Colossians 3:22-24, Ephesians 6:5-8). The book, *Your Work Matters to God*, by Doug Sherman and William Hendricks makes the point that work is a vital part of God's plan. He will repay us for whatever labor we do for others. Every time we punch a clock or show up at the office, we're working for two paychecks—the one from our immediate employer and the one from the Heavenly Master. According to Colossians 3:22-24 we are to work "with sincerity of heart

143

and reverence for the Lord. Whatever you do, work at it with all your heart, as working for the Lord, not for men, since you know that you will receive an inheritance from the Lord as a reward."

Abraham Lincoln had a lot to say about work. "My father taught me to work but not to love it. I never did like to work, and I don't deny it. I'd rather read, tell stories, crack jokes, talk, laugh—anything but work!"

Lincoln always loved to poke fun at himself, but when a woman wrote him about her two sons wanting to work, he replied, "Set them at it if possible. Wanting to work is so rare a want that it should be encouraged."

Charles Kingsley, an English clergyman of the 19th century, put it this way: "Thank God—every morning when you get up—that you have something to do which must be done, whether you like it or not. Being forced to work, and forced to do your best, will breed in you a hundred virtues which the idle never knew."[1]

THE PARABLE OF THE MINAS

How will God reward us for our stewardship of these things? Jesus told two parables about it. The first was the parable of the minas (Luke 19:11-26). A mina was a sum of money, amounting to one hundred denarii. Since a denarius typically equalled one day's wage for a laborer, we might calculate a mina was worth one hundred days wages, or about four thousand dollars in today's terms.

This nobleman gave each of ten slaves one mina, then went on a journey. When he returned, he reviewed each slave as to how he had done with his four thousand dollars. The first servant invested that mina and it yielded ten more minas. He ended up with $40,000. The master commended him, "Well done," and then gave that slave a new job: he would be in charge of ten cities. Why did he get this sudden raise? Because he was faithful in a small trust, the master knew he would be faithful in a larger thing, like ruling whole cities in his kingdom.

The second slave reported a similar story, only he made five minas and ended up with $20,000. The master commended him and made him ruler over five cities.

The third slave, though, didn't invest his mina at all; he hid it away because he was afraid of the master. Why was he afraid? Because the master was "a hard man" who took out what he did not put in and reaped what he did not sow.

We can draw several important conclusions about stewardship from this parable.

First, God expects us to invest what He gives us for Him. God doesn't give us the good gifts of creation simply that we might hide them away for our own pleasure. No. He wants us to invest them so that His work is advanced.

Second, since every slave received the same amount, there are certain things that all of us have in common. Life, for instance, or a single day, or the opportunity for an education, or a physical body. How we take care of these resources and use them for His work matters in God's eyes.

Third, every slave gave an accounting. The master wanted to know specifically what each slave did with what He'd given. Obviously, the first two slaves eagerly presented the results of their work. But the third one was reluctant. In the same way, there are those who may look forward to judgment—with both humility and excitement—because they long to show the Lord what they have done for Him. This is not sinful pride, but the joy that comes through seeing the good gifts of God influence others.

Conversely, there are those who will shrink away from the reality of judgment, suddenly fully aware that they wasted their lives, even though they were Christians.

Fourth, there were differing rewards. One slave got ten cities in the new kingdom. The second received five. The third not only lost what he had, but it was given to the one who labored well.

Fifth, the citizens of the country hated the master and refused to allow him to reign over them. I suspect Jesus meant that these slaves did not have it easy in that country. Investing their minas and getting a return would be difficult, though not impossible.

This parable pictures what it means to be a steward of God's gifts. He wants us to labor long, hard, and hearty as His stewards, knowing that our toil is not in vain. It's too easy as a Christian to look around and feel as though everything we do accomplishes little or nothing. What does it matter if I work hard in my garden or lawn? Who cares if I get regular checkups at the dentist; I could get away with fewer. And what difference does teaching juniors make? They're all rascals anyway, aren't they?

God rarely pulls back the veil of time to reveal the true impact of any of our labors. He reserves that surprise for eternity. But He also promises that wise investments in His work, excellent preparation in teaching, careful attention to our possessions, and every other form of stewardship never escape His notice. He's not "making His list and checking it twice"; rather, He knows every effort and guarantees to deliver just rewards and words of praise.

THE PARABLE OF THE TALENTS

Jesus also told His disciples another parable about stewardship. We call it the parable of the talents (Matthew 25:14-30). Let's look at some of the details of this parable.

1. The master "entrusted" his possessions to three servants while he went on a journey. It was like saying, "Here, take care of what I own and invest it as you see fit in line with the principles you know I believe. When I come back, I'll reward you."

2. In this case, each servant was given "according to his ability." To one he gave five talents, to another two, and to a third, one.

146

A talent was a sum of money by weight equal to six thousand denarii. In today's terms using the same formula as that in the mina illustration, we come out with $40/day x 6000, which equals $240,000. We're talking about a huge sum of money, not just a few dollars.

Each received "according to his ability." The word for ability is *dunamis*. It referred to each servant's special combination of mental, emotional, and volitional faculties. The master didn't simply give out his possessions haphazardly or thoughtlessly; he tailored his gift to each servant's personality and God-given qualities.

Similarly, in the matter of stewardship, each of us has been given a life in time and space. We are where we are because God put us there. We have what we have because God gave it to us. God chose, in His perfect wisdom, all-encompassing power, and infinite love, to endow us as He has. There is no mistake about who we are or what we have or where we are. We never need to lament, "If I only had such and such abilities" or "If only I was in a better situation" or "If I only had more time." No, those are simply the lines God has drawn to give us body, soul, and spirit. Now He wants to see how faithful we will be within those limits and with what He has given to us.

3. Each slave did something with his talents. One gained five more talents. The second invested his two talents and came up with two more. The third hid his master's money in the ground. It's interesting that he didn't squander it, or run off to the far country, or go out and buy something nice for his wife. But we'll talk about that in a minute.

The point is that each of us must invest the time, talents, and treasure God has given us. How we do that is up to us. God will not force the issue, though if we allow Him to, He will work in us for His glory. We can invest wisely, with our eyes always focused on whom we're really responsible to, recognizing that our master will come back and call us to account. Or, we can do something else, as the third slave did.

4. The master finally settled accounts with his slaves. In the end, the master came back and wanted to know what had been done with his possessions. Each slave had a chance to "show and tell." The master did this on an individual basis, reviewing each slave's work without respect to the others.

Similarly, the Scriptures assure us that God will "settle accounts" with each of us. He will "give to each person according to what he has done" (Romans 2:6). That settling of accounts involved...

> *...a chance for each slave to demonstrate precisely what he'd accomplished.*
> *...an evaluation by the master.*
> *...a personalized reward or punishment for what was done.*

The first two slaves wisely devoted their talents to doing good and came away with a great gain. The master praised them and rewarded them with greater authority and position in his household.

NOW, ABOUT THAT THIRD SLAVE

But that third slave didn't fare so well. Notice what he did.

He accused the master of being a "hard" man. The word means "stiff, harsh, stern." This slave saw the master not only as nasty, but unjust. The other slaves didn't see it that way. In fact, they were very eager to serve well. But this slave had a skewed, even sinister, attitude toward the master. Why? We'll see in a moment.

He was "afraid" of the master. So he hid that talent in the ground and gave it back to him without any other result. The word used for "afraid" is the same word from which we get "phobia." It can mean anything from terror to reverence.

In this case, though, I think this slave was lying! He wasn't afraid of the master at all!

Why do I say that? Notice what he did: he hid his talent in the ground. Why did people do that in those day? It was the only way, if you weren't rich, to secure something for safekeeping.

Why didn't this slave spend the talent? Because, so long as the master was alive, he did honestly fear him, or at least the consequences of losing the master's talent. He hid it in hopes that the master would disappear or die on his journey. Then he could keep the money for himself.

Still, why didn't he invest it anyway—just to see what would happen?

The answer comes out in the master's pronouncement: you "wicked, lazy servant!" That was it in a nutshell. He was "wicked." His heart was filled with malice. He didn't care about investing the master's money; he wanted it for himself.

He was also "lazy." The word means "sluggish" or "slothful." He simply wanted to get by until his big chance came along. He probably looked only for an opportunity to get rich quick. And this was it! So he was willing to wait around doing nothing, in hopes that the master would never return.

WHY AM I TELLING YOU THIS?

So why am I telling you this?

Because each of us can find ourselves in that parable. We're either high octane people who invest five talents and make five more. Or, we're lower octane folks who only get two and make two. Or, we're like the "wicked, lazy" servant who wiles away his days hoping to gain God's rewards without having to lift a pinky. He probably does not represent a true Christian, though that's not clear from the parable.

We can't push it too far. But when it comes to rewards, we must remember that God operates on the basis of perfect justice. We will receive "what is due...for the things done while in the body, whether good or bad" (II Corinthians 5:10).

Hopefully, this will sound an alarm and offer a word of warning. We can't squander the time and abilities God has given us in senseless pursuits. Nor can we sit back and hope somehow it will all come together someday.

No, we must make those hard choices. Some choices are

easy. But many choices require deep commitment, integrity, and morality.

During the Crimean War of Britain with Russia (1853–56), the British government approached Michael Faraday, the famed scientist, and asked if he could prepare great quantities of poison gas for use on the battlefield. Faraday replied immediately that the project was feasible—and he would have nothing to do with it![2]

Neglectful, complacent, wicked, self-serving stewards will lose out in the day of Christ. But conscientious, persistent stewards who faithfully take care of the gifts, possessions, and people God has entrusted to us will one day stand before our Lord and hear those words, "Well done, good and faithful servant." We cannot squander our wealth or abuse our family without incurring loss on a heavenly scale as well as the earthly.

Make your choices. Keep them moral as Michael Faraday did. Strive for excellence. Soar to the stars if you can. But if you find yourself slogging it out in the mud, don't fret. God sees it all, from the grime to the sublime. He rewards us one at a time, just as He give us opportunities to serve—one at a time.

FOOTNOTES
[1] Quoted in *Bits and Pieces*, (The Economics Press, Fairfield, NJ, August 1978), p. 5.
[2] Isaac Asimov, *Book of Facts* (Bell Publishing Co., New York, NY, 1979), p. 265.

-14-
Staying True to the End

Paul B. MacCready has built several manpowered aircraft over the years. On June 12, 1979, his latest invention faced its biggest test. On that day, Bryan Allen, a 137 pound American bicyclist and hang glider enthusiast, stepped aboard the "Gossamer Albatross," MacCready's second manpowered airplane. Its wingspan spread 93 feet, 10 inches. It weighed 70 pounds. Allen planned to pedal the bicycle-geared propeller and fly the plane across the English Channel, some 23 miles.

Fifteen miles across the Channel, Allen "hit the wall." He had drained his water bottle and suffered dehydration in the humid airplane compartment. He could hear messages through the radio plugs in his ears, but the batteries were down; he could not relay messages. *Albatross* dipped to within six inches of the waves.

Allen thought it was over. He couldn't go the distance. He signalled to the rescue craft that he was giving up and coming in.

But in pedaling to climb the ten feet necessary to slide aboard the craft, Allen suddenly noticed the air was calmer. With a burst of energy, he warned the boat off and sped for France.

The last quarter-mile, Allen said, "My legs started to get useless." But the apparition of a large fin in the water beneath him pushed him on. With only several hundred yards to go, his legs cramped. His body steamed with sweat. But he could see

151

Cap Gris-Nez, France looming ahead.

Pushing on fiercely, he cleared the beach. He landed moments later to raucous cheers and staggered out of the cockpit to accept a shy kiss from a female spectator. His first words were, "Wow...Wow!"[1]

I don't know anything about Bryan Allen's faith, but I believe he demonstrated a level of perseverance that any Christian can admire and emulate. Does God give any special attention to perseverance through struggle? Will there be special mention of those who endured through:

–tough marriages?

–searing financial troubles?

–loss of jobs, possessions, friends, and loved ones?

–heat, cold, fire, and storm to take the gospel to lost people?

Absolutely! "If we endure, we will also reign with Him," Paul says in II Timothy 2:12. Jesus told the church at Smyrna, "Do not be afraid of what you are about to suffer....Be faithful, even to the point of death, and I will give you the crown of life" (Revelation 2:10). Paul advised the Corinthians that an imperishable crown awaited those who ran and endured a disciplined race (I Corinthians 9:24-27). James said, "Blessed is the man who perseveres under trial, because when he has stood the test, he will receive the crown of life that God has promised to those who love Him" (James 1:12).

Persevering in the midst of trials, difficulties, problems, setbacks, setdowns, and setups is something God Himself applauds. When Jesus obeyed to the point of death, as Paul says in Philippians 2:5-8, God "exalted Him to the highest place." "Momentary, light affliction" in life produces something amazing for those who will enter the kingdom of God: "an eternal glory!" (II Corinthians 4:17). In other words, every time we "keep the faith," honoring Christ in our attitude and witness while slogging through distresses and difficulties, God piles up "glory" that will one day adorn us in heaven. How that will be manifested is a mystery. But the fact of it is as sure as Scripture.

WHAT IS PERSEVERANCE?

To persevere means to "finish the race" as Paul put it in II Timothy 4:6-7. It's being faithful to the end. It's doing right even in the face of threats, persecutions, loneliness, hatred, and scorn.

Among the many things God says about perseverance in Scripture are these truths:

•**No one can take us out of God's hand.** John 10:27-29. "My sheep listen to my voice; I know them, and they follow me. I give them eternal life, and they shall never perish; no one can snatch them out of my hand. My Father, who has given them to me, is greater than all; no one can snatch them out of my Father's hand."

•**God will see us through.** Jude 24-25. "To him who is able to keep you from falling and to present you before his glorious presence without fault and with great joy—to the only God our Savior be glory, majesty, power and authority, through Jesus Christ our Lord, before all ages, now and forevermore! Amen."

•**God intends to perfect us.** Philippians 1:6. "Being confident of this, that he who began a good work in you will carry it on to completion until the day of Christ Jesus."

•**God works in us to help us persevere in doing good.** Ephesians 2:10. "For we are God's workmanship, created in Christ Jesus to do good works, which God prepared in advance for us to do."

•**God is faithful and can be trusted to help us forge ahead.** I Corinthians 1:8-9. "He will keep you strong to the end, so that you will be blameless on the day of our Lord Jesus Christ. God, who has called you into fellowship with his Son Jesus Christ our Lord, is faithful."

•**Nothing can take God's love away.** Romans 8:38-39. "For I am convinced that neither death nor life, neither angels nor demons, neither the present nor the future, nor any powers, neither height nor depth, nor anything else in all creation, will be able to separate us from the love of

God that is in Christ Jesus our Lord."

•Staying true to the truth is extremely important in God's eyes. II John 8. "Watch out that you do not lose what you have worked for, but that you may be rewarded fully." Revelation 2:17. "He who has an ear, let him hear what the Spirit says to the churches. To him who overcomes, I will give some of the hidden manna. I will also give him a white stone with a new name written on it, known only to him who receives it."

Perseverance is both something we do, and something God accomplishes in us. Where we end and He begins is a mystery. The Bible warns us both to trust God to see us through and also to examine ourselves to make certain we're in the faith (II Corinthians 13:5), to make sure about His calling and choosing us (II Peter 1:10), and to recognize that we can't do it on our own (John 15:5).

THE IMPORTANCE OF PERSEVERING

Why is perseverance so important in God's eyes?

First, because it's the essence of faith and trust. Faith is not static. It's not a one-time event. A person is saved not because he "believed" way back when, but because he "believes" now. John 3:16 tells us that whoever "believes" in Christ has eternal life.

We do not put our trust in a "moment," the time "we went forward," or "prayed the prayer." It's not the action we trust; it's the Person—Jesus Christ. It matters little how many times we say we believe or go forward. What matters is that there is a reliance and trust on Christ NOW for that once-and-for-all decision.

The essence of faith is that you believe now and keep on believing. While many Christians go through periods of doubt and unbelief, real faith ultimately perseveres. It's dangerous to say a person is a Christian because he believed in the past—but isn't living that faith now. It may be that he's truly saved. But John repeatedly tells us in I John that real believers love the brethren, keep His commandments, and follow Christ. No one can fail repeatedly and permanently in these areas and also claim to be a Christian.

A second reason God wants us to persevere is because lifestyle speaks louder than wordstyle. Why did God test Adam and Eve in the Garden of Eden? Why did He test Abraham by requiring that he sacrifice Isaac? Why did He allow Satan to test Jesus in the wilderness? Why was Peter "sifted" to the point that he ended up denying Jesus three times?

Because it's through events and circumstances that God reveals to us our true selves and heart. It's simple to say, "I believe," or "I'm a Christian," or "I love God." Words come easily. What's tough is action—saying, "I believe" when those words may result in being shot or whipped or cursed. Rejoicing in God even after you've been emotionally battered by some person or group for your faith.

It's not that God doesn't know what we will do or what the condition of our heart is. He's omniscient. He knows us inside and out and then some. He knows today what we will do on January 6, 1995 or 2002 or 3278. He planned it all before He ever created the world.

But because we live in time and space, we demonstrate our beliefs by our actions. What we are is not measured by what we say, but by how we act.

Jesus pictures the principle in Matthew 9:1-8. There, some believers brought a paralytic to Jesus for healing. After they laid him down in front of Jesus, the Teacher said, "Your sins are forgiven!"

Instantly, several of the Pharisees reasoned that Jesus was blaspheming God, for no one but God could forgive sins. They thought Jesus was usurping God's place.

Jesus knew what they were thinking and confronted them. "Which is easier: to say, 'Your sins are forgiven,' or to say, 'Get up and walk'?"

Which was easier? In reality, neither. Only God can forgive

155

sins. Only God can heal a paralytic instantly. But in a sense, anyone could say the first. Whether it happens is not immediately verifiable. But if you said, "Rise and walk," your talk will get an immediate reaction. If the paralytic doesn't get up, then you've proved you're a fake!

So Jesus said, "But so that you may know that the Son of Man has authority on earth to forgive sins...." He turned to the paralytic, saying, "Get up, take your mat and go home." And lo and behold, that's exactly what the paralytic did.

Jesus backed up His words with His actions. He proved He had the authority He claimed by showing it in an obvious way.

In the same way, our faith is not borne out by our words as much as the context of our life. James said, "Show me your faith without deeds, and I will show you my faith by what I do!" (James 2:18). Persevering through life proves we're the real thing. If GM never puts it's new Klunk through a battery of road tests, how will the company know it can perform? If we don't run and debug a computer program, how can we be sure it functions properly? Enduring—staying with the faith even though the world tries to stifle it—proves we have the real thing—to God, to the world, to ourselves.

In March 1916, Norman Rockwell made his first two sales to *The Saturday Evening Post* at 75 dollars each. He was ecstatic. Moreover, the editor of the *Post*, George Horace Lorimer, approved three other sketches. Rockwell knew he was on his way. He labored enthusiastically on his third cover from the sketch. But when he showed it to Lorimer, the director suggested that the old man in the cover was too rough and tramplike. Could Rockwell redo it? Of course.

He reeled home a bit miffed, but he started a new canvas. Nonetheless, when he turned it in, Lorimer gave him more bad news. Now the old man in the painting looked too old!

Rockwell staggered home, truly discouraged, but he decided to paint tough. He redid the painting with a young man.

No! This time the boy was too small.

He got another model and tried again.

"No, not quite right!" was the reply.

Ultimately, Rockwell painted that particular cover five times before George Horace Lorimer was satisfied. After the fifth try, though, he accepted it. Rockwell breathed whole palettes of relief, wondering if working for the *Post* might really be worth it. But Mr. Lorimer later told Rockwell that he was testing him. Norman never confessed to him, though, how close he'd come to giving up![2]

In a way, that's what God does with us. He knows our breaking point. But He also wants to show us what we're made of and what kind of faith we have—the lasting kind, or the brand that fizzles, chokes, and wilts. Over the course of time He brings trials and tribulations into our lives to prove to the world, to the angels, to Satan, and even to ourselves that we have the right stuff.

The grand truth behind the doctrine of perseverance is that of faith, God's confidence in us guaranteed by His own nature. He who began a good work in us will "carry it on to completion until the day of Christ" (Philippians 1:6).

Satan buffets us; the world throws a right hook to the jaw, and we go down. But somehow we stagger back up and belt our way back. Problems in the home, office, and church assail us. We fall to the mat, crying out, "Help!" God sends some of His fearsome spiritual fire and we somehow find the strength to rise.

Other circumstances batter us. But suddenly we find our course, reach deep, and come up with the haymaker that sends our enemies reeling.

We may not feel like we're doing very well. We may even be wheezing, choking, and gasping for a last breath. But God says, "In all these things, we are more than conquerors through him who loved us" (Romans 8:37).

"More than conquerors!" Obviously this is someone who is far more than your average, everyday, garden variety conqueror. No, this is one who gains an overwhelming, astonishing victory that will go down in the Hall of Eternal Fame!

You might feel like you're caught on the ropes. Each breath comes in a labored wheeze of doubt and fear. Take heart! There's glory at the end of the grind, for God stands ready to receive you with the raised arm of victory and a crown that will never wear out.

FOOTNOTES
[1]"Odyssey of the Albatross," *TIME*, June 25, 1979, pp. 46-47.
[2]Norman Rockwell, *My Adventures As an Illustrator* (Doubleday, New York, NY, 1960). Used with permission.

-15-
Everything? You Mean Everything?!

In Matthew 19:29, Jesus offers these sobering words: "And everyone who has left houses or brothers or sisters or father or mother or children or fields for my sake will receive a hundred times as much and will inherit eternal life."

When I read a passage like that, I tend to think of someone who remains single and travels to the sweltering jungles of inner Brazil to spread the Good News. Or the doctor who leaves a lucrative practice to take healing and help to the indigent of Bangladesh.

But in all honesty, I'm not sure Jesus only meant this for those who forswear a million dollar salary for a single item diet of casava roots and a house full of cockroaches in order to qualify. Making any decision that trades comfort for discomfort in order to take the news of Christ to others certainly meets the requirements.

I think of a couple I know who left excellent jobs and a beautiful house to become missionaries in Germany, teaching in a seminary there. They now live in modest housing with limited provisions compared to what they had in the United States. He worked a fast-track job in the U.S. with a high salary and tremendous career potential. Yet, they discarded it all for the tough job of learning a new language, raising their own support, and struggling on a financial balance beam. Jesus says to that family, "I have a hundred times as much for you in the new kingdom."

I think of a young pastor and his wife who moved halfway across the country to take a church, even though it meant long separations from their immediate family. They're doing well, but the husband has had a hard time adjusting to the distance, the long waits between visits, and the climate. Has he made a mistake? Would it be better to settle for something else closer to home? No, to him Jesus says, "I have prepared a hundred times the family fellowship in heaven that you could ever have here."

I think of a doctor in a high-rung practice who has chosen to give much of the time he could be working to discipleship with businessmen, his church, and several Christian schools. It has cost him heavily in time and money. Is he a fool? No, the Lord assures him, "No matter what you gave up for Me, I will repay you a hundred times and more in the kingdom of God."

Is this a hype dream? Is it pie in the sky? Is it fool's gold?

In the eyes of the world, undoubtedly. But Christians see with different eyes. And those who make sacrifices for the work of God will be repaid personally by Jesus Himself.

KINDS OF SACRIFICES

What kinds of sacrifices count for eternity?

•**Leaving some valued person or thing behind in order to serve Christ.** This is what Matthew 19:29 is all about. Anyone who gives up something he would like to do—build a business, launch a career, buy a luxurious house—because he believes it's God's will to do something else, will be rewarded. It might involve giving up a secular group in order to spend time with the family. It might be refusing to go on a trip with the boys because you know it'll be nothing but drinking and dirty stories. One man might buy a cheaper car in order to donate more to the work of Christ. Another chooses not to go to certain movies or parties, because he believes they don't glorify God. It's doing anything "for Christ's sake" that is a sacrifice. That is, it costs you personally in some way.

•**Sacrificial giving.** When the widow dropped her two mites into the treasury, Jesus announced that she had given far more than anyone else....She, out of her poverty, put in everything— all she had to live on" (Mark 12:44). Giving off the top and keeping the rest costs little. But this widow, while the amount wasn't much, made a real sacrifice.

King David demonstrated the nature of sacrifice in II Samuel 24:20-25. David was offered free oxen for a sacrifice, and he refused. He said he'd pay for the oxen. Even when Araunah insisted he wanted to give the oxen to David without cost, David stood firm, saying, "I will not sacrifice to the Lord my God burnt offerings that cost me nothing" (II Samuel 24:24).

A real sacrifice costs. This is why tithing is not necessarily a New Testament concept. Giving to meet a need of God's church, however great the cost, is. That means a person may be called upon to give a major portion of his savings, or to cash in an insurance policy, or sell off stock, or do something else that in some way even puts his security in jeopardy, not just an easy 10 percent. Who is giving more—the person who makes $100,000 a year and gives $10,000 to the Lord's work, or the fellow who makes $10,000 and gives $1,000? Like the widow who offered her mites, the latter person may be making a real sacrifice, while the former is simply obeying a rule he thinks he should keep. Which pleases God? Only true sacrifice pleases God, not skimming off the top.

Does that mean we're to be foolish about our giving? No, we are to act in faith. When we attend a service and give in response to some tear-jerking plea, our emotions are piqued, but what about our heart? Often we later regret what we did in a burst of gooey feelings.

On the other hand, faithful giving has no regrets. We look to the Lord to meet our need, and then we give liberally and cheerfully, believing that He will take care of us, either now or later, whenever He deems best. Faithful, thought-out and prayed-through giving is not only realistic, it also pleases God.

•**Any gift, small or large, that takes time and effort.** Jesus says in Matthew 25:40: "I tell you the truth, whatever you did for one of the least of these brothers of mine, you did for me."

I am reminded of this truth when others demand my attention while I'm immersed in job or hobby I want to finish. My daughter asks for a sandwich or a glass of milk. My wife suggests I stop writing to assist her in the kitchen. A friend calls and spills out a problem or situation that needs counsel and encouragement. A relative or neighbor asks a favor that means I must spend my Saturday morning at their house.

A multitude of small and large needs clamor for our attention. How will we respond? Shut them all down with an abrupt, "No"? Sometimes it's right to say no, but many times it's also wise to say yes—out of love for them and commitment to Christ's plan for holiness, goodness, and kindness. When we do any of these "because we are Christ's disciple," God says He'll reward us.

It seems incredible, doesn't it? But Jesus wants us to think that all those intrusions and irritations and little attention-demanders can be worth something eternal, if we'll meet a need with faith and love.

•**The sacrifice of praise.** Hebrews 13:15 reminds us to continually offer a "sacrifice of praise" to God. We bring praise and thanks to God, just as the Hebrews brought burnt offerings as gifts of love to God.

How is praise a sacrifice? In this context, it's an act of worship, a gift, an action, something we offer to God as a way of rejoicing in His goodness and grace.

When you think about it, what can we really offer to God that could be valuable to Him? Money? He owns the whole universe. Works? He could turn stones into men who would work far harder than any of us. Service? Yes, He values our service, but in reality He can always find others to serve.

The one thing we can offer to God wholly of ourselves, freely and from the heart and soul, is praise. We can compliment Him, tell Him we love Him, bless Him for His mighty deeds, extol His perfections to others. No one can force that from us, not even God. When we offer it to Him, He is pleased and blessed.

Though confession of sin is important, God doesn't want our eyes on sin, but on Him. When was the last time you really spent time listing all the reasons you could think of for God's greatness, the fruit of His love in your life, and the glory of who He is?

•**Denying yourself.** Paul writes in Philippians 3:7-8 that everything he once thought important—his birthright, his position as a Pharisee, his zeal in keeping the law—were worthless next to knowing Christ and suffering with and for Him. He grasped the great truth of self-denial: When we give up personal satisfaction in order to spend our lives for another, we taste a much sweeter savor—the joy of self-denial.

Have you ever felt certain sacrifices you have made were a waste or useless, unnoticed or even spurned? When we give more money at times than we can afford out of genuine love and conviction, and then suffer hard times, it's easy to become bitter. "Why didn't God repay me?" we cry. When we set our lives on the line and suffer injury or even permanent bodily harm, it's not a long jump to feel, "God betrayed me! God didn't keep His end of the bargain!"

But God rarely repays us in this world for deeds and sacrifices given in secret as an act of devotion and worship for Him. At times they may seem foolish gestures, or the profligate splurges of a fool. People around us may even tell us we're getting just what we deserve for our "altruistic guilt-ridden actions!"

Nonetheless, God sees. He knows. Genuine sacrifice stimulates His highest praise (Luke 7:36-50 and John 12:1-11).

Look for opportunities to give. Then give, sacrificially, cheerfully, liberally, privately. God sees—and will reward.

-16-
I Guess Leaders Will Really Have It Good Up There

The Apostle Peter offered some extraordinary words of hope for those who lead in I Peter 5:4: "When the Chief Shepherd appears, you will receive the crown of glory that will never fade away."

The Chief Shepherd is Jesus. He promises to reward leaders with a "crown of glory" that will never grow dim with age or be forgotten. Glory will be the signpost and billboard of every life in heaven, yet God says leaders will receive a special notation of His love and joy in their work.

THREE QUALIFICATIONS

Still, this gift is not without its qualifications. Just being a leader of God's people is not enough. Peter spells out three requirements that go with this crown.

First, he must be a "willing" overseer. Peter says in verse two of chapter five, "Be shepherds of God's flock that is under your care, serving as overseers—not because you must, but because you are willing." The expression, "not because you must" literally means "not under compulsion." No one forces this person to enter into the work.

Frequently, people take positions of leadership "under compulsion." The pastor or another leader "wangles" them into it, either by making us feel guilty if we don't, or giving us a strong emotional appeal that communicates, "If you don't do it, who will?"

Nonetheless, Peter advises us to serve "willingly." The word means "intentionally, voluntarily, of his own free will." This person makes an unalloyed choice. No one argues, threatens, cajoles, or incites him into it. In some cases, others may approach him and employ such tactics to persuade him. But in the end, the decision was his own. He did it willingly, even gladly.

Second, he must not be "greedy for money, but eager to serve." We've seen so much of the former in our generation that often it's hard to believe anyone could lead and minister out of sheer joy and "eagerness." Yet, God desires that leaders exhibit this sense of vitality and enthusiasm.

The word for "eager" is interesting. The Greek is *prothumos.* *Thumos* is a common Greek word for anger but it also means "fire and passion." A person full of *thumos* expresses passionate, all-out, total commitment, one who stops at nothing to accomplish God's will.

However, *prothumos* intensifies the passion. *Pro* means "before," or "in front of." It suggests a higher rank than other forms of the same thing. Peter is saying, "Attack your ministry not just with normal passion, but with passion of the first rank, the kind that is so obvious everyone sees your commitment is to God." It is to this person that God promises a crown of glory.

Charles Spurgeon, the great 19th century prince of preachers, pled, argued, coaxed, and implored his listeners to come to Christ, to listen to the message, to accept the truth. Someone once asked him, "How can I become a preacher like you?" Spurgeon replied, "Take a bottle of kerosene, strike a match, and people will come to see you burn!" He held nothing back. He gave his all. He marshalled every argument he could think of. He struggled to make the gospel as clear as possible.

Similarly, I like listening to a number of radio pastors. They often make me smile the way they stop in the middle of a sentence and say, "Listen now! Listen! Now listen to this!" They cry out for a verdict. They demand your attention.

That's the kind of passion I think Peter means. If you're going to lead, then get into it—not for the money, but for the glory—the crown of glory!

Third, Peter says they must not lord it over those entrusted to their care but prove to be examples. We've all seen how some people manage to "lord" it over others. They bark their orders. They throw fits when people don't respond. They demand loyalty, submission, abject attention, unwavering commitment.

Adolph Hitler required that. Some time ago I read that when he didn't get his way he often fell to the floor and literally chewed on the edge of the carpet! When people bucked his orders, he exterminated them. He wanted all the cheers, all the accolades, all the admiration, all the power.[1]

A true leader, though, is an "example." The Greek word here is *tupos*. It means "type" or "image." Two important New Testament words illustrate the idea. The first is *xaracter*. It's found in Hebrews 1:3 where the author says that Jesus is "the exact representation" of God's being. This word refers to an original image imprinted onto the face of a coin. The picture that remained was called the *tupos*, the type.

Similarly, Jesus as the *xaracter* stamps us with His image. We become the *tupos*—a type or picture—of Him that others can see. Leaders function precisely the same way: They are pictures of Jesus to the others in His flock. Paul expressed the same idea when he said, "Follow my example, as I follow the example of Christ" (I Corinthians 11:1).

Is it arrogant for a leader to say that to his flock? In some cases, undoubtedly. If the leader does not reflect Christ's example but tells you to be like him anyway, that's conceit, ego, pride.

But in other cases, godly men and women provide wonderful

166

portraits of what it means to follow Christ. When we see someone living a godly life, they become an object lesson of how we should also behave. We can apply the truth in our own circumstances because we've seen how another used it in his life.

One of the most eloquent examples of a great leader is George Washington. Why is he considered the father of our country, and one whom people revere, love, and honor?

Because he was one of a very few, rare men whom power could not seduce or corrupt. As a country, the United States can thank the God who raises up kings and leaders that George Washington was no Xerxes, no Hitler, no Castro. Even Thomas Jefferson, who often disagreed with Washington, eulogized him with respect and honor. Jefferson said,

"...His character was, in its mass, perfect, in nothing bad, in few points indifferent; and it may truly be said that never did nature and fortune combine more perfectly to make a man great....His integrity was most pure. No motives of interest...friendship, or hatred [biased] his decision. He was...in every sense of the words, a wise, a good, and a great man."[2]

Example teaches. It guides. It provides a graphic picture of how to do what we need to do. But even more, it stays with us throughout our lives, reminding us of the way that is eternal, the truth that is sure, and the life that is glory...or vainglory.

WARNINGS

But as wonderful as these promises are for leaders, the Scriptures contain some stern warnings to those who lead.

1. Leaders will give an account. Hebrews 13:17 reminds us that our leaders will give an account to God of how well they led us. That's enough to give anyone pause. But more than that...

2. Leaders and teachers will receive a "stricter judgment." James 3:1 advises us to think long and hard before becoming teachers. That raises not only the rewards but also the requirements. Teachers will answer not only for what they taught, but for how well they lived out what they taught (Matthew 5:19-20). In God's eyes there is no such thing as "do what I say, not what I do." Telling and not doing is not only wrong, but God will judge those people all the more severely.

3. The eternal destinies of others is, in many ways, dependent on a leader's accuracy in telling the truth. Paul told Timothy that as he persevered in his ministry and continued to be diligent in his life and doctrine, he would "save both [himself] and [his] hearers" (I Timothy 4:16). He advised him to be diligent and accurate so he would not be ashamed (II Timothy 2:15).

Error in transmitting the truth is extremely serious in the eyes of God. That means no teacher or preacher can approach the Word of God lightly or with a disdain for study. Accuracy is paramount (II Timothy 2:15). While no one is infallible, and honest errors can certainly be forgiven, God cannot overlook laziness or lack of diligence in study, preparation, and proclamation.

God spoke even more firmly to Ezekiel, telling him that if he did not warn others of the consequences of their sin, God would hold him accountable for their blood (Ezekiel 3:18). That principle surely applies to leaders today who fail to study and proclaim the Word of God accurately.

4. Leaders do their work before God, Jesus, and the elect angels. Paul charged Timothy to remember that his ministry was carried on in their sight (I Timothy 5:21). Angels witness all we do. They're watching and even learning from our example (Ephesians 3:10). We lead, not just before a class or congregation which is scary enough, but also before the whole spiritual world.

5. Leaders must have a "treasure" mentality about God's Word. Paul commanded Timothy to "guard the good deposit" or "treasure" that he had given him (II Timothy 2:14). Anyone who teaches the Word on any level has been entrusted with God's treasure—His Word. It's the most valuable thing in this world. Nothing compares to it because it alone can open the door to eternal life. We enter that door through knowledge of the Word: "Faith comes from hearing the message, and the message is heard through the word of Christ" (Romans 10:17).

Anyone who hears and believes the gospel possesses that treasure. To withhold it from others is tantamount to refusing bread to a starving man. To abuse, twist, change, delete, or add to it brings down the wrath of God (I Timothy 1:18-20; Revelation 22:18-19).

6. God requires that leaders be singleminded in their devotion to Him. Paul warned Timothy that no soldier "gets involved in civilian affairs—he wants to please his commanding officer" (II Timothy 2:4). If anyone desires to lead others to the Lord, he cannot do so on a part-time basis. I don't mean that literally, but in the sense that we can't straddle the rail or play half in and half out. Either we're ministers of the gospel where God has placed us, or we're involved in the world. But we cannot serve God *and* money.

7. Leaders can lose rewards if they tolerate error. John warned his readers in II John 8, "Watch out that you do not lose what you have worked for, but that you may be rewarded fully." The context specifies tolerating deceivers. Christ rebuked the churches at Pergamum (Revelation 2:12-17) and Thyatira (Revelation 2:18-29) for allowing false teaching to flourish in their midst. In the church today, the willingness to "live and let live" and the toleration of rank error in the name of "being kind, gentle, and peaceable" have no place. That doesn't mean we become violent with heresy, start "witch-hunts," or initiate another Inquisition. But God does demand that we name the error, confront it, and, if it's not repented, follow the process of church discipline until the one committing the error is no longer recognized as a Christian (III John 9-12; Matthew 18:15-17).

8. Leaders are called to care about people. Peter told us not to lord it over people, but to be examples. It's astonishing how many leaders care nothing about those under them. They're stuck on themselves. Their inflated egos crowd everyone else out of the room.

Fortunately, many leaders show they care in inspiring ways.

During the fifth and last game of the 1970 World Series, the Cincinnati Reds hit the bottom of the ninth inning with two out, no one on. They were losing 9 to 3. Big Hal McRae, the leading hitter for Cincinnati during that Series, stalked up to the plate. Strangely, Cincinnati's manger, Sparky Anderson, pulled McRae from the spot and sent in Pat Corrales, the back-up catcher to Cincinnati's star, Johnny Bench. He hadn't played a single inning in the Series and was not known as a great batter. To many, Anderson's decision invited certain doom.

Corrales walked to the plate and smacked a grounder to Brooks Robinson. Robinson rifled the ball to first base, and the Series was over.

After the game, reporters jostled in the clubhouse as Anderson explained his decision to the hushed team members: "When you're a back-up catcher behind Johnny Bench, most people don't know you're around. But Pat Corrales helped me, never complained, and encouraged the other guys. I knew that this might be the only chance in his life for Pat Corrales to play in a World Series. I'm sorry he didn't get a hit, but I'm very glad I have him the chance."[3]

That's leadership.

THE STRUGGLE

Things like confrontation, witnessing, accuracy in exposition, and the plain hard work of walking with Christ sometimes stagger those who must lead by example. But that struggle—which I'm sure all leaders face—doesn't mean that we shouldn't try and keep laboring and growing in Christ. It doesn't mean that we should shrink from the task, give up, or bow out, calling ourselves "unqualified." Or give in to fear (II Timothy 1:6-7). God desires honorable leaders; and He honors those who lead in an honorable fashion.

Leadership also brings with it consistent and debilitating problems—with people, with buildings, with organizations, with the government, with money. Many leaders feel as if they go on not from glory to glory, but from headache to headache.

Leadership does bring on headaches, stomachaches, and heartaches. But God assures us over and over that how we labor as leaders and examples, how we expend ourselves, how we give and love, is never void or useless. We may not see immediate results. We may never see any results. But God understands the conditions under which we work. He places us in them, and He rewards us individually and comprehensively. We can't compare ourselves to others, for He won't. We needn't worry that we're not making waves; sometimes only a ripple is what He wants.

William Carey (1761-1834), sometimes called "The Father of Modern Missions," worked many years in India, compiling dictionaries and translations of the Bible. He often spoke of himself as a "plodder." He didn't sprint out of the gate and make his mark in a hundred yard dash. No, he staggered along, reeling from shock to disaster, but in the end, his life counted for so much. His constant prayer—as ours should be—was "God make me a plodder."

We forge the golden medals in the here and now. Don't look on the sprinters and hustlers with envy. Plod along. Practice the truth. Live out God's will. He will reward you as only He can do.

FOOTNOTES

[1]William L. Shirer, *The Nightmare Years* (Little, Brown & Co., Boston, MA, 1984), pp. 345-346.

[2]Esmond Wright, *Washington and the American Revolution* (English University's Press, Ltd., London, England, 1957), p. 187.

[3]Cited in *Reader's Digest*, Frank Slocum, "Personal Glimpses," (Pleasantville, NY, October 1980), #9, p. 32.

-17-
Little Things Are Big Things

When people send me gifts, usually I respond enthusiastically and with gratitude. Frequently they'll answer: "Oh, it's just a little thing." Or, "It was the least I could do." Or, "It was no trouble. I'm glad you like it."

But such "little things" mean a lot. They communicate love, friendship, appreciation, joy. In fact, the more I think about it, the more I realize that "little things" are a big part of life. A word, a note, a pat on the back, helping an elderly person out of a car, visiting someone who is sick, bringing lunch to a shut-in, counseling someone over the phone, being "nice" when you're not in a particularly "nice" mood all add up. The "stuff of life" is largely insignificant single moments that add up to a full-blown portrait of who we really are.

What does God say about some of the little things in life?

WORDS

In Matthew 12:36-37 Jesus warned His disciples through all the years that we'll give an account of every word we've spoken. The statement comes off as a warning about idle, foolish words. But the principle of reward leaps out of the truth. We will "give an account." When we stand before Jesus, He will ask how we used our tongue. Did our words edify or did they petrify? Did we build up others, or squash them down? Were we masters of sarcasm, or givers of grace? Did we think before we spoke, or did we speak without thinking?

God sees our words as incredibly important. With them we can benefit others and meet needs (Ephesians 4:29). An apt, thought-through reply offers the listener joy, says Proverbs 15:23. They fill the speaker with good, if he uses his tongue for good (Proverbs 12:14). God establishes "truthful lips forever," according to Proverbs 12:19. The tongue has the power of life and death (Proverbs 18:21). Reckless words pierce like a sword, says Proverbs 12:18. And a gentle answer turns wrath away (Proverbs 15:1). Proverbs runs over with wisdom about our mouths.

But James also speaks at length about our tongues in James 3. The tongue, though small, can set aflame masses of people just as a single spark can destroy a centuries-old forest.

Perhaps the best principle of all is found in Hebrews 10:24-25. The author commands, "Let us consider how we may spur one another on toward love and good deeds." How? Certainly spoken encouragement, praise, an exhortation, a compliment are high on that list. We've all seen the results of tongues that gossip, spread rumors, lie, slander, and abuse others verbally. God has, too. God will require an accounting of every instance of such behavior.

But at the same time, we will also receive great rewards for using our tongues in godly, uplifting ways. We may forget what we said, but others don't, and God never could.

Is your tongue used for good, for edification, for love, for encouragement? Every word adds up. Use your words like goblets of gold.

MOTIVES

A second not so little thing in the eyes of God is our motives. Paul says in I Corinthians 4:5 that God "will bring to light what is hidden in darkness and will expose the motives of men's hearts." Paul warned us not to judge one another on the basis of assumed motives. God will bring it all out, so leave it in His hands.

Motives are a tricky item. When I look within myself, I nearly always see a mixture. I see both good motives and selfish or even bad ones lurking behind the same deed. For instance, my daughter asks me to stop writing and listen to something she wants to tell me. I might feel irritated about it initially. I'll tell myself it's right and good to give her my attention. Next, I'll flinch back a spark of resentment toward the Lord that I have to pause in my work to do this. Finally, I'll end up firing aloft a mental prayer of confession and thanks that I have an opportunity to listen and that I have a daughter who wants to talk to me.

What was my true motive? I'm not sure, but I'm convinced He can sift it through and see the overall motive behind any actions in a life of commitment and faith.

Next, there's the problem of changing motives. I might give a hundred dollars to an organization out of love for the Lord at the time of deposit to the plate. Three days later, though, I could feel the pinch and regret it because I can't pay a bill. A day after that I confess my sin in the matter. And then two days later I sense the same twitch of resentment again. In the end, I dismiss the whole thing, forgetting even to confess my sin.

Again, what was my real motive? Did the resentment negate the praise and joy?

Finally, there's the problem of ambivalence. A person can honestly be pulled in different directions in a situation. He might stall giving an answer, but in the end he does what's right, though reluctantly. For instance, employees might expect a raise for work well done. The Christian boss grimaces over the impact on his profit or the bottom line, then gives the raises, generous and fair ones. Deep down he knows it's right and good. But even though he prays about it and confesses a lousy attitude, he still can't work up a "hallelujah," a joyful noise, a rendition of "Majesty," or even a resigned nod toward heaven.

But he still does what was right despite a poor attitude and stingy feelings. Does he get any credit from God for that?

174

Frankly, I don't know how to sift through it. Or how God will. But one thing is sure: the Lord will do what's just and fair, and that's enough for me. My responsibility is to work on my attitude, confess wrong motives, strive for integrity, do what He expects of me, and walk humbly before God.

The important thing about motives is that we concentrate on our own and forget trying to figure out what lurks in the hearts of others. Each answers to God individually.

The Christian fights this struggle inside of himself every day. Is he doing it for the money, the ministry, or self? Is he doing it to get someone off his back, or out of a genuine desire to help? Was she conscious of trying to please the Lord, or just being "nice" because that was the easiest way to deal with something?

How often are our prayers clogged with mundane and selfish thoughts like, "Please make this record sell, Lord," and "I sure wish you'd let me win the Lottery, Father," or "Can you please make that kid shut-up?" Even kneeling at our beds, we can be smitten with nasty and negative thoughts.

Ultimately, though, I believe the Lord watches us for obedience. Doing what is right comes first. Our desire to honor Him forces us to persevere in the struggle against a sinful nature. As we grow, we gradually learn to do what's right for godly reasons with a completely righteous attitude.

LONGING FOR HIS COMING

Another little big thing is simply wanting—even longing—for Jesus to come back. Paul says in I Timothy 4:8 that he expected to receive a crown of righteousness. But more than that, he assured us that that crown was reserved not only for him, but for all "who have longed for his appearing."

Sometimes I ask myself, "If you could choose between the following, today, which would you choose, Mark?"

1. Suppose you could choose between the guarantee of publishing a novel that would become the #1 New York Bestseller for a whole year, or the coming of Jesus right now—

which would it be?

2. Suppose God offered you the opportunity to speak next year before a million people at one shot with tremendous applause, and the coming of Jesus this very minute—what would you want?

3. Suppose God told you to choose between living a long life here on earth full of riches, glory, honor, and prestige, with every good thing earth offers, and Jesus coming in the next second—what would you do?

Maybe I'm a little strange, but I do think about those kinds of things. Obviously, it's just a game. But it does help me pinpoint something inside myself, and that is how much I want Christ to come.

Recently, I taught a Bible study on the subject of heaven. One of the men in attendance, an ardent Christian, commented that heaven was a difficult concept for him. He confessed that he thought little about it. If Jesus came now, that was all right with him, and if He didn't, he was having fun, so it didn't bother him.

In my mind, it was a typical upper middle class American response. He was honest, yes, but the fact is that many Americans who also claim to be Christians have little motivation about their eternal future. In fact, as I solicited publishers about this book, several turned it down because the idea of "heavenly" rewards was not "practical" and "real" enough to most people. One editor even asked me if I would consider doing something on rewards "in this world," that is, how God rewards us right now for good works.

That attitude, unfortunately, stems directly from the fact that so many of us expect an immediate return on our investments. Why should we look forward to a "better" world? The one we're in right now isn't so bad! In fact, we're having a great time! Furthermore, why should I do "good deeds" for some ethereal reward "up there in heaven" when I can make $5,000 or $50,000 now?

The attitude that loves this world and prefers it to Jesus' work will gain nothing in His kingdom. Only those who have *truly* longed for His coming, not just as an escape from personal misery, will be rewarded with the crown of righteousness.

Going back to my three questions of a moment ago, I have to admit that the idea of a bestseller, or standing before a crowd to receive public acclaim, or living the life of a billionaire is pleasurable. But having Jesus come today is far, *far*, **far**, FAR preferable. Who cares about glory in this world? It's nothing. It will all fade away. What of its luxuries, its chocolaty pleasures, its glittering jewels? They're cheap imitations of the real thing and few of us ever partake anyway. They're nothing next to the overstuffed storerooms of eternity.

The cry of every Christian heart must be, "Even so, come Lord Jesus!" Those who make that cry their own will not only find a waiting Lord in heaven, but also a welcoming Friend laden with rewards.

NOTHING FORGOTTEN!

One of my favorite verses of Scripture, which I've already referred to several times, is found in Matthew 10:42: "If anyone gives a cup of cold water to one of these little ones because he is my disciple, I tell you the truth, he will certainly not lose his reward."

While that truth speaks worlds of hope to those of us who will never make the *Guinness Book of World Records*, speak before thousands, live in the pages of *Encyclopedia Britannica* or *TIME Magazine*, win a Nobel Prize, Pulitzer, Cleo, or Grammy, it also reminds us that:

–no deed, however small or great,

–no word, however simple,

–no thought or motive, however fleeting,

is forgotten, discarded, ridiculed, or scorned in heaven.

It all counts. And it will all be rewarded by Him whose rewards are the only ones that do count!

You may feel that your life adds up to little. You may suspect that when Christ gives out the crowns, you'll be lucky to get a bread crust. You may believe in your heart of hearts that Jesus will need a heavenly magnifying glass to find anything worthy of mention for you at the *bema*.

But it's my hope that you see the promises that everyone of us can live lives now that glorify Jesus, win His pleasure, and assure His acclaim. We can speak those soothing words if we'll only try. God will send us a multitude of fragrant opportunities to do good, if we'll only step up to the tape and run *His* race. The Lord can fill our hearts and minds with those anthems and songs of praise, if we'll only give His Spirit control.

No one has to live a useless, forgotten life. No, the things we do now can count. Every day can be filled with godly deeds, words of kindness, thoughts of love. We can be ourselves, and as we live out God's will, we can become all He created us to be.

Don't Give Up!

-18-
God Intends To Get Us There

The idea of a final accounting for every Christian terrifies most of us. That it may be public for all to see trembles even the stoutest chin. That the All-Knowing will Himself examine us in detail might cause us to run for the sticks.

But there are no sticks to run to. Nowhere to hide. And it doesn't matter how much we tremble, the day will still come.

What will it be like?

Above all, it will be a day of reward and rejoicing. God's purpose is not to shame us or bring us into heaven with distraught faces and tearful eyes, but to present us "without fault and with great joy" (Jude 24-25). He wants to dispense not one or two but billions of those crowns of glory, life, and righteousness. He plans to award multitudes of "white stones" and "hidden manna." We can look forward to a day of loving, gracious words, not stern rebukes.

Just the same, we might ask, how can it be? As any of us looks back on our lives to date, we might shiver, trying to find something we think is truly worthy of heaven's rewards. Charles Spurgeon, sure. And Augustine, John Wesley, Martin Luther, John Hus—naturally. Also, any from the Bible–the widow with her two mites, Paul, Peter, Mary and Martha, Mary Magdalene, Joseph and Mary. Then there's Isaiah, Noah, Noah's wife, Sarah and Abraham, Deborah, Joshua and Caleb, Isaac and Rebekah, Jacob and Leah and Rachel.

But me and you?

"Well, I did teach Sunday School, but I haven't heard from those kids in years."

"Yes, I invited people over for dinner now and then. But Bill didn't make much money, and all we had was meatloaf and macaroni."

"I did raise my kids in the knowledge of the Lord, but they've gone off now and sometimes I wonder if they believe at all. One of them has rejected Jesus completely."

"I guess I'll just have to settle for a dusty little shelf somewhere. Frankly, I'll be glad just to be there."

Do we really care *why* we do the things we do to live for Christ here on earth?

FOUR POTENT WORDS

If that's the way you see it, then let me give you four powerful words of cheer.

First, God is working in us right now to make sure that when we get there, it won't be a day of doom and tears. Ephesians 2:10 says that we "are His workmanship." Philippians 2:13 reminds us "it is God who works in you to will and to act according to His good purpose."

In other words, while we're responsible for our deeds and behavior, God is also sovereign and working in us. Day by day He leads us, sometimes subtly, sometimes boldly to give us the opportunities and character traits that He will one day reward us for.

While a teenager, my dad told me that if I made Eagle Scout, he would pay for me to go to Philmont Scout Ranch in New Mexico. Philmont offers the greatest camping experience any Scout can encounter. But I had a long trek ahead of me, some eleven merit badges and lots of hard work.

But it wasn't as though Dad told me the end without getting involved in the means. He helped me as I worked on those merit badges. He encouraged me. He even coached me a bit and helped find the people necessary to approve my work. He asked me repeatedly how close I was and attended the quarterly banquets that gave out the awards.

Come that summer, much to my astonishment, I made it. Although I hadn't actually received the award, I had completed all of the merit badges. It was only a matter of the end of the summer ceremony. Dad sent me on the bus to New Mexico with a smile and a handshake.

While an earthly Dad can assist like that, our heavenly Father has far more power at His disposal. Not only does He give us the directions and leadership in His Word, not only does He encourage us through the people in the church and elsewhere, not only does He shows us how to reach our goals through training and teaching sessions, but He actually comes and dwells inside us, working from the inside out to produce that legacy of goodness, growth, and character that He Himself plans to applaud.

God gets involved from beginning to end in our salvation. He hasn't left us on our own, giving us commands from afar. No. He comes right down to heart-rock and transforms us at the very core of our being until the true light shines through in all we do.

Second, He is able to present us before Him blameless. Jude 24-25 says, "To him who is able to keep you from falling and to present you before his glorious presence without fault and with great joy—to the only God our Savior be glory, majesty, power and authority, through Jesus Christ our Lord, before all ages, now and forevermore! Amen."

Jude's statement, "Him who is able" literally means, "He who has the power."

To what? "Guard" you from falling and "make you stand" before Him "unblemished with exultation." Not only does He guarantee never to let us fall (to the point of losing our salvation), but Christ will also present us to the Father without blame. That happy moment will be sanctified, holy, perfect, and we will be worthy of honorable mention for we shall be like Christ.

One of my college teachers used to say, "The purpose of teaching is not to eliminate the flunkies, but to enable all to succeed. A good teacher takes a student and helps him grow throughout the year until he presents him at the next level, ready for even higher performance."

Even the best teachers sometimes fail in that lofty calling, but God cannot fail. Precisely where God's working in us ends and our part begins is never spelled out in Scripture. But He enables each of us to succeed on an eternal scale.

God works in us and also expects us to work with Him. God transforms us, but we must accept change. God empowers us, but we must yield to that power. God leads us, but we must follow. Scripture proclaims that He is sovereign, and we are responsible, exercising our wills without coercion from Him or others.

Some might say that's a contradiction. How can God be both sovereign and we be totally responsible at the same time?

The problem is not the human logic of it, but an understanding of the power and mind of God. He works in ways that we can't comprehend because we don't possess His omniscience. He possesses the power to control all events, deeds, words, and thoughts, and at the same time to allow everyone apparent and complete freedom. How? It's part of the majesty and glory of God. It's part of the reason we worship and serve Him. His thoughts are not our thoughts, and His ways are not our ways (Isaiah 55:8-9).

Third, God's promise is to perfect us. The promise of Philippians 1:6 reminds us, "He who began a good work in you will carry it on to completion until the day of Christ Jesus."

That's powerful. God is at work in you—in me—every day. Even though at times it may look like He is doing nothing, He continues to toil in every life to complete His grand design.

A friend of mine named Frank Chilcoat works as a newspaper driver for the *Baltimore Sunpapers*. He's a thin, wiry fellow with sharp blue eyes and a face reminiscent of a craggy Paul Newman. For many years he struggled with alcoholism. But in his late fifties he became a Christian. I worked with him and his wife, Frieda, teaching them how to have a quiet time and to walk with Jesus.

Frank told me one morning as we sat down that he'd been a little late the previous day on his *Sunpapers* route. He pulled into a Dunkin' Donuts to fill up the newspaper box and found the handle of the box smeared with a jelly donut. Frank said, "The guy must have come out to get his paper and when I was late, he got mad and tried to get back at me by smearing the jelly donut. But, you know, God must be changing me. Ordinarily, I would have gone into a rage about that, and would have been miserable the whole day. But this time I didn't. I just laughed, went into the Dunkin' Donuts, asked for a wet rag, and cleaned it up. That's not normal for me. God's doing something in me, now I'm sure."

Another friend I worked with was an ex-drug-user and jailbird named Mike. He's an imposing guy with a scarred face, barrel chest, and the strength of a Grizzly bear. I befriended him for nearly a year before he finally accepted Jesus. He began to change in many ways, from controlling his anger to speaking gently with his wife. One day he said to me, "It's like I'm the same person I always was, but inside I'm different. Like I have a whole new outlook. But at the same time, I'm more Mike than I've ever been in my life!"

That's the beauty of God's perfecting work. While he changes us, he makes us more ourselves than ever before.

Fourth, God is faithful. First Thessalonians 5:24 tells us, "The one who calls you is faithful and he will do it." Second Timothy 2:13 adds, "If we are faithless, he will remain faithful, for he cannot disown himself."

Both of these verses illuminate a potent truth: God cannot give up on us, leave us, be disloyal, or even disown us. While we may fail, make mistakes, and even rebel at times or run off to "do our own thing," He simply cannot wash His hands of us. He won't forget. He won't leave us. Though the story of the Prodigal Son portrays a father who let his son go to the far country and had to wait for him to make up his mind to return, the other side is also true. In the parable of the lost coin and lost sheep, the owner seeks his own until he finds them.

God continually runs after us. He is committed to our growth, our training, our equipping, our sanctification. He wants to give us His eternal acclaim on the day we stand before the Judgment Seat of Christ.

I always liked the story I read in *Our Daily Bread* of a master sculptor who repeatedly applied the finishing touches to a bronze. He filed, scraped, and polished each surface until it glowed. Then he filed, scraped, and polished some more. Someone asked him, "When will it be finished?" The sculptor replied, "Never. I just keep working until they come and take it away."[1]

That's the faithfulness of God. He keeps working and working until they come to take us away, or Christ returns, whichever comes first.

IF THIS IS TRUE, THEN...

If this is all true, then...

•**Forget what is behind.** Paul told us in Philippians 3:13 that he forgot what was behind and pressed on toward the goal.

We all make mistakes, even waste the opportunities of our Christian lives. Do you know what God says about it? If you sinned, confess it, then move on (I John 1:9; John 21). Forget what's behind. It's gone. It's done. You can't change it. Plunge on into the future with new resolve to follow in a way that honors Christ.

That's the ultimate joy of the Christian life. Everyday starts fresh. Every week offers new opportunites. Today really is the first day of the rest of your life. That is never so true as in the life of the believer. Whatever's gone before doesn't matter to God. We can start walking with Him now.

•**Press on.** While Paul forgot what was behind him, he also pressed on. He forged ahead. He kept on moving.

I've observed that there are three stages to commitment. The beginning is a time of fun, determination, sweat, blood, tears, and joyful toil in the trenches. It's almost a frolic. We love what we're doing. As a new Christian, I experienced this joy and exuberance. Witnessing, even with rejection, thrilled me. Prayer, Bible study, church fellowship—I thrived on them.

But then comes a second stage. It's as though those who disagree with you suddenly become the mortal enemy. You tolerate no one who refuses to go along with every jot and tittle in your theology. You battle those who offer the smallest differences of opinion. You even proclaim that some people can't be born again because they're not in your group, your denomination, or in agreement with your interpretation of the Bible.

Finally, though, there's a third stage. You realize for the first time that you're probably not going to cut a wide swath in church history, leaving your fingerprints all over everyone. That's the place where the real saints are made. Instead of slinging off for the North Woods or soaking in an acidic bath of bitterness, they hang in there, muddle through, teeter by. The Christian life, if anything, is a struggle, a fight, a sweaty side-aching race, a marathon. You wheeze for breath. The finish line is nowhere to be seen. And everyone seems to hurtle by you, without a pain or a misstep. But somehow you plod on.

At this point, pressing on requires plain, gut-wrenching commitment. There's no visible end in sight. But it's out there, and even now the Lord gives you the strength to keep on moving toward it.

•**Don't lose heart.** Paul said in Galatians 6:9, "Let us not become weary in doing good, for at the proper time we will reap a harvest if we don't give up."

Years ago, when I slogged through one of the hardest trials of my life—a biochemical depression that nearly made me give up the faith—I reached a point where I felt so low I prayed that God would kill me. As I neared graduation from seminary, I faced the coming days with terror. I believed I'd be a failure.

One afternoon, while driving back from the store at the beginning of Christmas vacation, I poured out my feelings to my mother. She listened kindly, but I could tell my self-defeating words made her angry. She said, "Mark, I'm telling you, you have what it takes. I've watched you grow. I saw you go through high school, with all its struggles. You survived. I watched you work through college. I remember all those moments of indecision, girl problems, career problems, worry about grades. But you made it through. You survived and graduated."

I listened intently. She was right. I had survived. But...

"Now you're ready to leave seminary and start a career. Sure, there will be struggles and setbacks. But I tell you, you won't fail. If you try, you can't fail. And even if you have a setback, as long as you get up again, in the long run you'll succeed. That's what counts."

I looked at her and shook my head. It sounded great. But my mind was still dark. "But I'm afraid I'll just be a washout."

I could see the rising fury in her eyes. "All right. I'll tell you what. I've been reading a biography of Eleanor Roosevelt. Her husband, Franklin, also was afraid of failure. It came down to the last few days before he had to decide to run for governor of New York. He hadn't done anything. She asked him why. He was in a wheelchair. People were saying nasty things about him. It would be a real fight. She knew it. And he knew it. He said, 'I'm afraid I'll fail.' Do you know how Eleanor answered?"

I shook my head.

" 'Then don't!' she said. 'Don't fail.' "

She let the words sink in. "Mark, you're afraid you'll fail. My word to you is, 'Then don't.' Give it all you got, and as long as you don't give up, you won't fail."

I sat there stunned, a lump squeezing my throat. I couldn't say anything. I just nodded.

Encouragement like that got me through seminary and through numerous difficulties that threatened to throw me afterward.

The Lord also counsels us, "Do not lose heart. What you're doing matters. Stick with it. One day I Myself will reward you."

•**Be steadfast and immovable.** First Corinthians 15:58 concludes Paul's great sermon on the subject of our coming resurrection. He says, "Therefore, my dear brothers, stand firm. Let nothing move you. Always give yourselves fully to the work of the Lord, because you know that your labor in the Lord is not in vain."

Stand firm. Don't be moved away from the truth.

Give yourselves.

WHY?

"Because...your labor in the Lord is not in vain."

Whatever we do, however big, small, or in-between, whether we achieve worldwide recognition or fail to get notice even in our own households, no matter whether we had mixed motives or were dead concentrated on serving the Lord with all our heart, soul, mind, and might...IT'S NOT IN VAIN! God remembers. He will reward.

I often turn to Ann Kiemel Anderson's story from her first book, *I'm Out To Change My World*. In it, she relates how she grew up in Hawaii where she, her twin sister, and her brother were the only light faces in a sea of dark faces from Japan, Africa, China, and India. All through her high school years she cried herself to sleep each night wishing she was someone else. She hated the insults of Hindus and Buddhists as they ridiculed her God. Repeatedly, she asked her father, "Daddy, why does it pay to serve Jesus?"

He'd only reply, "Hang in there. It pays."

In the morning she'd beg her mother not to send her to school. But her mother only pushed her out the door with the words,

"Don't you know that life is made up of ordinary days when there's no one to pat you on the back? When there's no one to praise you? When there's no one to honor you? When there's no one to see how brave and noble you are? Almost all of life is made up of ordinary days. And it's how you live your ordinary days that determines whether or not you have big moments. Get out there and make something of your ordinary days."

Ann would stumble out the door in tears.

Then came the day of her graduation. She and her sister sat nervously on the platform to receive some awards for their high grades. They both won scholarships, but she knew no one had ever heard of Northwest Nazarene College.

She watched as each student stood to receive his award. Slight applause followed and that ended it. She reviewed the four years of pain, bitterness, fear, and doubt, wondering if it had all been worth this. Then the principal called Ann and her sister, Jan. He said, "We're Hindus and Buddhists, but these two girls came and brought their God to our campus. They've changed our world."

Ann writes that she could, "only remember the applause and that it never seemed to end." All the pain and doubt fled. In her heart she whispered, "Daddy, you were right. Through all the thousands of ordinary days when I wanted to give up, it paid. It pays to be true. It pays to follow Jesus."[1]

Few of us will do anything that the history books record and praise. Many of us get our names in the paper only as an obituary of two or three lines. Committees will pass us over for the awards. In most cases, we won't even be considered. Even our own great-grandchildren will forget us. I don't know my great-grandfather's first name.

But there's only one Book that matters. What God writes in that Book will never be forgotten. There's only one name that matters—the one He calls us by.

I look forward to that day—not with an arrogant confidence

that I shall receive great applause or accolades—but with the knowledge that He intends to get all of His own there, blameless, pure, and ready for an eternity that will glow on from glory to ever greater glory.

It doesn't matter what the world thinks, says or does with us. All that matters is that we practice the things that count.

What really counts?

Living out His will in thought, word, and deed. Doing good. Obeying His truth. Worshiping, loving, serving, sacrificing. For Him. All else is dust, babble, and rubble.

The time will come. He'll inscribe His name on our foreheads. We'll see His face. He will crown us. We'll wear rubies, emeralds, and diamonds more resplendent than the crown jewels of England. He Himself will set them on our heads. And finally we'll bow, cast those crowns at His feet, and cry, "Worthy art Thou, our Lord and our God, to receive glory and honor and power!"

The moment will surely arrive. We'll stand before Him. Only what He says matters now will matter then. Invest your life in that, and, in the end, your life will count forever.

FOOTNOTES
[1]Richard DeHaan, "It Takes Time." Taken from *Our Daily Bread*, (Grand Rapids, MI: Radio Bible Class, 1981). Used by permission.
[2]Ann Kiemel, *I'm Out To Change My World* (Impact Books, Nashville, TN, 1974), pp. 27-29. Used with permission.

About the Author:

Mark Littleton is a graduate of Colgate University and Dallas Theological Seminary. He lives in Columbia, Maryland with his wife and two children. *Life from the Inside Up* is his twelfth book. His two previous books with Accent were *Submission Is for Husbands, Too* and *When God Doesn't Follow* Your *Plan. Life from the Inside Up* is also a one or two day seminar that Mr. Littleton offers through Winsun Ministries. If you are interested in that or other seminars from this ministry, you can write the author at:

> Mark Littleton
> WINSUN MINISTRIES
> P.O. Box 278
> Hunt Valley, MD 21030.